SMART GUIDE TO REAL ESTATE

Rent To Own

Investor's Edition

by Gary Hibbert

www.SHCInvestor.ca
Copyright

Library and Archives Canada Cataloguing in Publication

Hibbert, Gary, 1974-
    Smart Guide to Real Estate. Rent to Own: Investor's Edition
/ Gary Hibbert.

Issued also in electronic format.
ISBN 978-0-9880794-0-3

    1. Real estate investment. 2. Renting to own. I. Title.

HD1382.5.G54 2012   332.63'24   C2012-905034-2

SHC Publications
P O Box 51109
Rossland/Harwood
Ajax, ON
L1T 4S0

Note to the reader: This publication is sold with the understanding that
neither the author nor publisher is engaged in rendering legal, accounting
or other professional service. If legal advise or other expert assistance
is required, the services of a competent professional person should be
sought.

Printed and bound in Canada

Note to Reader continued

The information contained in Smart Guide to Real Estate. Rent to Own Investor's Edition is meant to serve as a comprehensive collection of time-tested and proven strategies that the authors of this guide have applied to substantially increase their monthly passive income revenue on www.shcinvestor.ca. Summaries, strategies, tips and tricks are only recommendations by the authors, and reading this guide does not guarantee that one's results will exactly mirror our own results.

The authors of Smart Guide to Real Estate. Rent to Own:Investor's Edition have made all reasonable efforts to provide current and accurate information for the readers of this publication. The authors will not be held liable for any unintentional errors or omissions that may be found.

The material in this guide may include information, products, or services by third parties. Third Party materials comprise of the products and opinions expressed by their owners. As such, the authors of this guide do not assume responsibility or liability for any Third Party Material or opinions. The publication of such Third Party materials does not constitute the author's guarantee of any information, instruction, opinion, products or service contained within the Third Party Material.

Great effort has been exerted to safeguard the accuracy of this writing. Opinions regarding similar website platforms have been formulated as a result of both personal experience, as well as the documented experiences of others.

No part of this publication shall be reproduced, transmitted or resold in whole or in part in any form, without the prior written consent of the author. All trademarks and registered trademarks appearing in Smart Guide to Real Estate. Rent to Own: Investor's Edition are the property of their respective owners.

Table of Contents

Introduction

This book is a step-by-step guide on how to rent a home for top dollars as an investor. Many new investors get into Real Estate with the full intent to be investors and end up becoming landlords.

When I say landlord, what I'm referring to is running around fixing leaky faucets, changing light bulbs, cutting lawns and collecting rent cheques each and every month. You didn't get into Real Estate investing to become a "Jack of All Trades". I imagine you got into Real Estate to create additional streams of income and to live life to the fullest. If you are like most investors, you got into Real Estate to get out of the 9-5 rat race and to stop living pay cheque to pay cheque.

This guide offers a step-by-step process that I have used to fill all of our properties as well as other investors that I have worked closely with. By following these steps, you too can fill your home for top dollars, receive large deposits before handing over the keys, attract great tenants and at the same time create a win-win scenario for both you and your tenant (who we like to call *future homeowner*).

Features and Icons Used in This Book

Throughout this book you will see icons below. I've added these to help draw your attention to important and very useful information.

Watch for margin notes like this that highlight key information for you to pay attention to

"Why isn't my home being rented fast enough?"

"Am I doing what needs to be done?"

"What if it doesn't work?"

I have had days like these where I ask myself hundreds of questions, and it stressed me out in the beginning. This is why I decided to write this easy to follow guide to show you exactly what to do, but more importantly, to enjoy what you are doing.

One of the most important things I have learned is, once you have systems and processes in place and they work, don't change them. By doing this, you can almost guarantee success by duplicating your process over and over again until it becomes second nature.

It is also very important to track what is happening while you are renting your home. Imagine tracking calls, knowing that if you have 20 calls, 10 will book an appointment, 5 will show up, and 2 will be serious candidates. It's almost like being able to forecast when your home will be rented. How exciting is that?!

I don't have all the answers however, I do have the experience, a great team behind me (lawyers, accountants, mortgage brokers), and have dug myself out of some deep holes. I do mean deep!

What has helped me through the tough times is my core team, who has stuck together during the rough times, stayed focused on our goals, and continue to motivate each other. You see, when you hang around great people, their energy can't help but rub off on you. As long as 2 or 3 people can agree upon a common goal, nothing is impossible. Remember that!

This is not a get rich quick scheme but a way to secure your financial freedom within the next 10 years. Now I know 10 years may seem like a long time but if you look at the previous 10 years, how fast did they pass? I would recommend planning for your future today and taking the necessary steps to start working on your dreams right now.

The only time you can do anything is NOW! The past and the future are only an illusion. Think about it.

You can't do anything to change the past, and to affect the future you have to act NOW. The purpose of life is not what you get, but what you become.

FACT: Did you know that approximately 70% of all millionaires make their money through Real Estate?

What Is Rent to Own?

So what exactly is Rent to Own? The process works similar to leasing a car. Renters (a.k.a. *future homeowner*) pay a certain amount each month to live in the home and at the end of the term (usually 2 to 3 years) can purchase the property from the seller at a pre-determined amount set at the beginning of the term.

Generally, prior to the tenant moving into the home they pay an option fee (usually 3% of the purchase price) plus first and last month's rent. In order for them to be in a position to take possession of the home within the next few years, they will need to build on their initial deposit to acquire the Bank's required 5% of the agreed upon purchase price of the home. In order to accomplish this, a portion of their rent (called rent credits) goes towards the down payment which is accumulated on the initial deposit (option fee) when the tenant first moves in. In many cases the rent premiums for Rent to Own homes are an amount slightly above the market rent price with a portion of that money going towards the down payment of the home.

Keep in mind that the tenant has the option to purchase the home; this is not an obligation. In other words, if the tenant decides to walk away from the home after the term is up, they have the right to do so. However, if they exercise this option they will forfeit any deposit they put down and all rent credits saved over the agreed upon term.

For many families that are tired of renting and want to get into home ownership, this is a great option if they are having difficulties saving for the full down payment or have run into credit issues and need some additional time to restore. This is also a great option for the owner of the property as they will generally receive higher than normal rental fees. They will have a future homeowner who will be responsible for maintaining the home, including lawn mowing, snow removal, and all minor repairs (generally under $500). Why would a tenant want to be responsible for all this additional work and be willing to do it? It's simple. They know that in the next few years they will be the owners of this home and that is what you call a win-win scenario. The tenants wins because they are becoming a homeowner within the next few years. The investor wins because he remains an investor and doesn't need to provide typical landlord services, receives monthly cash-flow and a payout within the next few years to reinvest into additional properties to accumulate additional wealth.

Let's go through a typical Rent to Own example: A house is worth $250,000 and typical market rent in the area is $1,500 a month. Someone who's renting to own might pay $1,700 -$1,800 a month in rent and then receive a $200 rent credit each month. Then you add the option fee, in this example let's use $6,000. With a typical 3 year lease, the future homeowner would earn $7,200 in rent credits. Adding the earned rent credits to the initial option fee, the renter has a total of $13,200 for a down payment.

What Can I Expect From This Guide?

> This guide is going to provide you with all of the information that you need to rent your home for a 20% - 30% higher price than a regular rental property.

I will give you the tools that you need as well as a comprehensive plan to follow that will have a suitable tenant ready to move into your home in a reasonable amount of time. Remember, I have used every suggestion in this guide and have filled homes time and time again, attaining deposits from $5,000 up to $20,000 before our future homeowners move into their new dream home.

What do I mean by a reasonable amount of time? On average, based on my experience, I would say between 4 to 6 weeks. Now, don't hold me to this. I have seen homes take longer to rent and I've also seen them rented much faster.

> Here is the key to your success in 1 short phrase.
> Beautiful homes in beautiful neighbourhoods!

The 2nd most important phrase is **location, location, location**. This is said 3 times not because the person who coined it had a stuttering problem, but because it is also a very important rule to remember.

Now before we jump right into how to rent your home successfully, I want to share with you a quick story and a few important points about the power of Real Estate and how Rent to Own can be an impressive system if carried out fairly and correctly.

When I first started working in the corporate world, I loved it, but after a few years of salary increases and added responsibilities my employment income hit a plateau. I could not maintain the lifestyle

7

Ask Yourself...What is Riskier?

So many people believe that Real Estate is risky business, but is it? The right question to really ask is this...

> "Is it riskier to have 1 to 2 streams of income or
> to have multiple streams of income coming in
> each and every month?"

To illustrate how powerful this concept is, have a look at the two pictures below.

What would happen if one of those streams in the picture on the left were to vanish? Do you think that life in that stream would be impacted significantly? The riverbed would not completely dry up however, life would have a much more difficult time trying to survive.

The one on the left is yours and your significant other's income and the one on the right is both your incomes plus your rental properties' income.

When you get to the age of retirement, I don't want to see you cleaning floors or working at minimum wage jobs to make ends meet.

Instead, my goal is to teach you, motivate you, and help you step-by-step on the best way to properly invest in Real Estate.

By using our proven techniques, we know that we can dramatically change your life in a few short years. If you take these ideas and get started today, the wealth you can build will allow you and your family to be financially secure for the rest of your lives.

> "If you work hard at your job you can make a living, if you work hard on yourself, you can make a fortune."
>
> – Jim Rohn

By owning Real Estate as an investment vehicle, you are not solely relying on your Canadian Pension Plan or your RRSPs. When my wife was working at a bank, she saw so many people ready to retire or already in retirement leave her office frustrated or crying.

Why?

To clarify, it was of no fault of hers, they were upset because they were only able to take out a certain amount each year or else they were going to get penalized heavily in taxes.

Now, I'm not making this up to convince you to get into Real Estate. I'm telling you this because it opened our eyes to where we were and where we didn`t want to be when we retired.

I'm not saying these are bad sources of income; my wife and I own RRSPs too. I just want you to understand that having passive monthly cash flow from your investments is a powerful source of additional income.

By owning properties, you are securing your future financial security and not just hoping for the best. Building your wealth is simple, but it's not easy. The thought of buying 2 homes and renting them out is simple. But actually doing it can be difficult unless you have a *Smart Plan.* I will show you how simple and rewarding Real Estate investing can be as well as the pitfalls to avoid.

Fact: The size of your success will never exceed the size of your belief.

Rent to Own Works in Any Economy

If the economy is in a downward trend, people have financial concerns and this strategy allows them to get into a home while prices are low. When the economy is climbing and home prices are soaring, Rent to Own (RTO) gives families a chance to get into home ownership if they were not able to get approved via the conventional way through the Banks.

Another great protection is to know what your buyout price is going to be in the **future** by setting the price **today.**

Rent to Own helps you to generate higher cash flow on a month-to-month basis and gives your tenants a chance at home ownership.

Here's the bottom line. If you had to pick from the 2 choices below, what would you prefer?

- Landlord or Investor?
- Renter or Future Homeowner?

It's Not Earth Shattering, but it's Important

What causes some people to become financially secure and successful?

This was the question I asked myself almost every day before I made some huge changes in my life and the way I looked at what I was doing. The first thing to realize is there isn't a quick fix to this question or a single secret...it's a formula. Success can't be acquired overnight, but it can happen with a gradual change in course direction, which is no different than readjusting the sails of your boat.

When I was in my early 20's I always knew I wanted to be successful but kept getting caught up in chasing the next shiny stone that caught my attention. By doing this, I was led down yet another path towards a get rich quick scheme.

So What Changed?

It was discovering that I did not have to blaze a new trail. All I had to do was find an existing trail to success, read the blueprint and follow it. It was as simple as that. Let me share with you some formulas that high achievers have in common. Trust me when I say this, it is not earth shattering, but it is very important.

Plan for the Day

I put this one at the top because I sincerely believe this is one of the most important steps of the day. Before you can take action you need a plan. Once your day is outlined, it takes all the stress out of trying to organize what is going on in your head. So don't start your day until you have your list completed. By doing this, you are now changing from being reactive to proactive. I find that by making your list the night before, your mind helps you to problem solve while you sleep. Then at the end of the day, week and year, make sure to review your progress.

Become Valuable

The more valuable you become, the more the marketplace will reward you. Become known as a resource and expert. The more you give the more you will receive in return. Your value is directly linked to your knowledge and your willingness to help others to achieve their goals.

Making Mistakes

Now I'm not saying that you should go out and deliberately make mistakes. What I am saying is don't be afraid to make mistakes, because they're the best teacher out there. I always tell my kids that there are no such things as mistakes, there are only learning opportunities, and new experiences. The key thing to remember is to learn from them.

Hang Out With the Right People

My mother had a saying when I was younger. "Show me your closest friends, and I will tell you who you are". In other words, associate yourself with the right friends and stay away from the ones that will drag you down. The ones who do not want to see you succeed are the ones who continually tell you that your idea won't work and who talk you out of taking chances. The people you hang around with... is who you will *become*.

Take Responsibility

We all blame others to some degree. The thing with blame is that it has a strong tie to success: *The lower your degree of blame, the higher your degree of success*. Get the job done, take responsibility and do not blame others if you fall short or things do not work out. People who are successful take responsibility for everything they do and everything that happens to them.

At the end of the day, there's nothing earth shattering about the points above. I'm no saint and from time to time I slip however, the more you practice these principles the more they become automatically ingrained within you. Before you know it, they're part of your life and become second nature to you.

5 Types Of Cash Flow
To Help You Start Creating Multiple Streams

> Get paid in 5 different ways from 1
> Rent to Own property.

If you're not familiar with the different streams of income that this investing strategy brings me month-to-month, year-to-year, don't skip this topic. Remember, when investing, the key is not to speculate but to get into an investment that will bring you cash flow during good times and bad.

1. **Down Payment** - Prior to our tenants moving into any of our homes, a down payment is required. The down payment received ranges in price. For most of our homes we have received between $5,000 to $20,000. For this example, let's use $7,500. That works out to approximately $200 a month when factored over a typical 3 year lease.

2. **Monthly Positive Cash Flow** - At the time of writing this book, most of our rental properties are bringing in a minimum cash flow of $350 each month and that's just for 1 investment property! You can take this extra cash and do whatever you want. Take the family out for dinner, watch a movie or maybe go to a basketball game.

3. **Mortgage Loan Reduction** – I also call this Equity Building. What I'm referring to is each and every month your tenant pays you rent, they are paying down your mortgage. Let's say on a home that cost you $250,000, depending on interest rates, the monthly loan reduction could be in the range of $500 - $600 a month. Every dollar of the loan that is paid down is wealth to

you. In fact, your tenant is paying off your debt. (See example on bottom of page)

4. **Appreciation** - Each year you own this rental property, its value will continue to increase. If your $250,000 home appreciates at 5% a year, your home would be worth $281,216   after three years. That is a $31,216 increase that becomes another income stream. If I divide this amount by 36 months, it would amount to approximately $867 each month.

5. **Tax Savings -** At the end of the year, your rental property could show a loss on paper for tax purposes. However, the reason is that the Canadian Revenue Agency(CRA) allows you to include a number of expenses throughout the year that can be included on your tax return (always consult your accountant). Let's say that the tax reduction saves you $1,000 in taxes. Divide that by 12 and it would total $83 a month.

If you add up these 5 income streams, the actual totals on a monthly basis would be as follows:

Down Payment:	$208
Cash Flow:	$350
Loan Reduction:	$600
Monthly Appreciation:	$867
Monthly Tax Savings:	$83
Total Monthly Return:	**$2,108**

Is It Possible to Have a Win-Win Scenario?
"Do for others more than you do for yourself"

Now many of you have heard this saying before but, how many people actually follow this great teaching from the Golden Rule Book? It's better quoted as, *"Do unto others as you would have them do unto you."*

When we first got into Real Estate investing we were involved in straight rentals. We knew that once we started investing that real estate would allow us to retire comfortably and provide us with the lifestyle we were looking for.

The strangest thing was that after a year of implementing a lifelong dream of investing we realized that the approach was good however the reward was only one-sided....OURS!!

We changed our thinking and investing strategies to encompass a WIN-WIN scenario for both us and our tenants.

Landlord Wins / Tenant Wins

The Rent to Own program is based on a WIN-WIN!! We rent our homes with the intention of helping the tenant to buy the home at the end of the lease period. The tenant has to have something on the table to lose, and they must have something at the end of the rainbow to create this scenario.

Attracting the Right Tenants to Your Beautiful Home

1. Size Does Matter

Understand that someone looking to get into a starter single-family home is usually moving from a cramped apartment building and is hungry for space. You do not need to purchase a rental property that is 2,600 sq. ft. however, 1,600 sq. ft. is much better than 800 sq. ft. Also, if your home is large enough, your tenants will not feel the need to move to have more space, which increases the probability of them purchasing your home during the lease period.

2. A Beautiful Neighbourhood

Everyone wants to live in a beautiful neighbourhood with a nearby park, close to schools, amenities and in a child-safe community. If your future homeowner feels insecure or the area is not a good place to raise a family, you will have a difficult time renting out your home. Remember, everyone wants to feel safe, see their neighbours looking after their properties, and know that they live in a great community.

Factual

Here's a chart representing the Bank of Canada's interest rates from 1975 to present day:

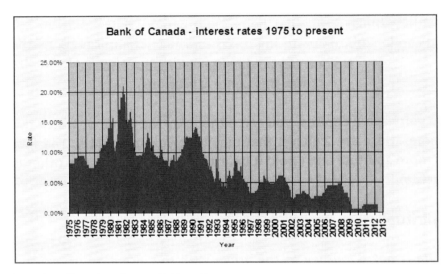

Source http://www.bcrealtor.com/d_bkcan.htm

Let's go further back in time.

Not too many people know what rates looked like from 1935 to 1955.

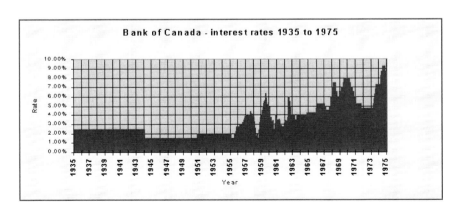

Notice anything strange from 1935 to 1955? Rates were incredibly low for a very long time. They stayed that way right after the Great Depression for almost 20 years! Is it possible that we could be in for the same thing as a result of the recession that we are currently experiencing?

I'm a firm believer that history repeats itself. Can we predict 20 years of low interest rates again? Like I mentioned earlier, no one has a crystal ball, but understanding the past can help you make educated decisions for the future.

> With this program we have seen homes yield
> monthly returns of over 30%.

To reiterate, this program is not a get rich quick scheme. If that's what you are looking for, you've joined the wrong program.

This guide is about a turtle that constantly beats the rabbit by using simple management systems, consistency, and by never taking their eyes off the prize.

Now, I will say this, it *is* possible to replace employment income with real estate income streams within the next 3-5 years if you work hard and apply our strategies. Just follow the principles in this guide and be fair to your tenants, a.k.a. future homeowners. Remember, what goes around comes around... I'm speaking from experience.

What About Financing?

This is probably the biggest stumbling block for most first-time investors. The question is usually something like this:
"I want to get into Real Estate investing, but to purchase a typical rental property the start-up cost for a home in the $250,000 range is close to $55,000. How do people afford this?"

This was probably the biggest hurdle for me when I first decided to turn to Real Estate investing. My wife (Darlene) and I were living pay cheque to pay cheque, trying to save for our children's education and put a bit away for retirement. Now we had to try to come up with almost $55,000 to buy only 1 home!

So how did we go from 0 homes to multiple homes in just a few short years? Our incomes didn't drastically change. I did receive a $1,500 raise but inflation surpassed that so I actually lost money. I haven't touched any of my RRSPs. The kids' RESPs are still accounted for and *I haven't hired any hit men!*

Looking back at where we were and where we are today, it was quite simple. However, when you are in the same state of mind that 80% of our society is, it's not so simple. You can't learn these things from your friends at work by the water cooler, or from your negative aunt or uncle who says they are trying to protect you from sure disaster because you will lose your shirt in Real Estate.

Here's what we did:

1. We slowly started to change the people we associated with.
2. We used very little of our money for investing.

Top 5 Things to Do When You Get Your Home

1. Clean the property thoroughly. Hopefully the previous homeowners left the property in good condition and all you need to do is a quick sweep, mop and vacuum.
2. Make sure all of your appliances are in good working order after the previous owners have left.
3. Check to make sure the furnace is working and turn on the A/C (if you have one) to make sure it is also in good working order.(if its not during the winter)
4. Make any required repairs that can be seen to the naked eye, such as nail holes in the wall, leaking faucets, blown out light bulbs, etc.
5. If there were major repairs that were observed during your home inspection, make sure these are completed prior to showing your home. If you are a handy man, great! If not, make sure you get a good contractor that can professionally do the work for you.

> Now that your home is ready for its first showing,
> make sure to get a lockbox.

You don't have to get a lockbox but for me, it was a requirement. I cannot tell you how many times I would show up to the property with 5 people lined up to see the home and I forgot the keys at my home. Ouch!!

To overcome this costly issue, I bought a lockbox. Let's say you and your partner or spouse is carrying out this Rent to Own transaction together and one of you can't keep the appointment. With a lockbox, you don't need to go home first to get the keys or worry about meeting your partner somewhere. You can go right to the property. It's a great time and cost saver and I highly recommend it.

Step #2 – Determine Your Price

The next step is to determine the rental price and the buyout price of your home for the next 3 years.

How to Determine the Rent Price of Your Home

To determine the rental price of your home, take a look in your area and find out what other homes are renting for. Once you are able to determine what the fair market value is, add an additional $100- $300 on top of that.

I'm able to justify asking for a higher rental price because I know I own a property that will be in high demand since it is a beautiful home in a great location. Remember, if you wouldn't move into it, don't buy it.

Example

Let's say you have determined that the starting price for your Rent to Own home will be $1,700 a month. When you market your property on and offline, list it at $1,600 which is the fair market value for your home. By doing this, you will attract more tenants to your home and create an auction for your property.

> The goal is to get as many people to view your
> home at the same time as possible.

The more people you can attract, the better your chances are of renting your home for top dollar.

People are emotional purchasers and when they see how beautiful and how much in demand your property is, they'll want to have it!

Once they arrive at your property, explain to them that the market value is $1,600 however, Rent to Own starts at $1,700. When they understand that you will be saving them $200 each month from this price, explain to them that in actuality they are paying only $1,500, which is less than market rent. You are essentially providing a forced savings for them.

Example of what to say

"I'm sure you can save $200 a month on your own, however, if you're anything like me, I open up a savings account, and 6 months down the road my account has increased quite nicely. I need a set of winter tires or I need to take a vacation and I end up dipping into my savings account. By embarking on a Rent to Own situation, the money is automatically being saved each and every month without you having to worry about it."

In almost all cases they will agree with this statement.

Another key point to remember is to give them an option.

You want to generate higher cash flow for your home than other properties on your street.

Using the example from above, allow them to have an option to pay $1,800 a month in rent and give them back $400 in credits.

At first this didn't make sense to me. Why would I want to give them so much in return? The name of the game is **cash flow!** The $400 is not actually coming out of your pocket but is subtracted off the buyout price of your home.

How to Determine the Buyout Price for Your Home

The next step is to determine what your buyout price is going to be. There are a number of different ways to appreciate your home however, you don't want to overprice it and scare people away. I prefer the 5%, 4%, 3% appreciation rate however, you can use a 4%, 4%, 4% or 5%, 4%, 4%...this is up to you.

I prefer the 5%, 4%, 3% appreciation rate because it is less between year 2 and 3 which is atractive to your tenants and over the years they are most likely going to purchase the home.

Example

Let's say you bought your home for $250,000. Here's an example on how to appreciate the home:

Purchase Price	= $250,000	
Appreciation		
Year 1 = 5%	= $262,500	
Year 2 = 4%	= $273,000	
Year 3 = 3%	= $281,190	

Remember that these numbers are all negotiable when you are at the table with a potential tenant. I have no problem altering the rent price or changing the credits or even the buyout price. Just make sure that the numbers make sense and are fair for everyone involved.

Remember, the final price will determine if your tenant will actually buy your home. Don't be greedy and set an unreasonable buyout price.

Step #3 – Creating the Savings Program

This is the actual savings program that we use for our properties. To determine the buyout price, subtract the initial down payment from the amount of credits saved for your tenants for what year they are ready to purchase the home.

Savings Program
Address: <u>for any city, anywhere</u>
<u>Current Property Value: $275,600</u>

Please select which savings program you would like to register for. Credits will be automatically earned towards the down payment of your beautiful home in your beautiful neighbourhood. You can move in now and your monthly house payment will earn you and your family hundreds of dollars towards your down payment and the purchase of this home. There is no obligation for you to purchase this home, but it is an <u>option</u>.

Savings Programs	Market Rent	Regular Savings	Super Savings
Household payments	$1,600	$1,700	$1,800
Monthly credits earned	$0	$200	$400
Monthly Rent	**$1,600**	**$1,500,**	**$1,400**
Credits earned in 1 yr	$0	$2,400	$4.800
Credits earned in 2 yrs	$0	$4,800	$9,600
Credits earned in 3 yrs	$0	$7,200	$14,400

Year 2 Buyout Prices

Regular Savings		Super Savings	
Monthly Rent	$1,700	Monthly Rent	$1,800
Monthly Credits	$200	Monthly Credits	$400
Total Rent Credits	($4,800)	Rent Credits	($9,600)
Option Down Payment	($5,000)	Option Down Payment	($5,000)
Purchase Price	$286,624	Purchase Price	$286,624
Final Price	$276,824	Final Price	$272,024

444

You may be asking, what does the 444 at the bottom of our form mean? This is what I use for internal purposes and how I track what I'm currently using for the appreciation rate. 444 simply means that I'm using an appreciation rate of 4% each year.

Since I may have multiple properties on the go at any given time it makes it easier for me to track. When you are first starting out, you will most likely only have 1, so you will probably not have to use this.

I've heard of some people using 7x7x7 appreciation rates.

> If there is only one thing you learn from me, please let it be this: Don't be greedy! There is more than enough money to go around for everyone!

If you manage this program correctly it can truly be a win-win scenario for everyone.

For example, I owned a home that I purchased a few years ago. We appreciated it at 5x5x5. At the end of the second year the tenants were in a position to purchase the home. At that point the value of the home was approximately $7,000 less than the original appreciation. During their residency, they looked after my property, I had next to no calls, and every time I visited my rental property it was in immaculate condition and they were always on time with their rent. I remained an investor not a landlord so why would I not negotiate a fair price with them?

Of course I would! It was the right thing to do. I helped them to restore their credit and they were fantastic tenants. I still walked away with a decent profit and more importantly, I helped a family to become homeowners.

> We accomplished our goal by being investors and we helped a family to become homeowners.

Step # 4 – Advertising and Making The Phone Ring

That is one of the most important things I have learned when advertising my homes.

Put yourself in the person's shoes who is reading your advertisement. You want to catch their attention with the description of your home. What is going to make your ad stand out from your competitors' advertisements?

There are a number of different ways to do this:

1. **Write Rent to Own** – Make sure your advertisement has the words Rent to Own in it. You want to catch their attention and let them know that you have a beautiful home that they can own in a few years.

2. **All Credit Scores Welcomed** – By including this, you are letting people know that you are willing to work with them. If you have someone that is going to give you a $5,000 deposit plus first and last month's rent, it means they are trying to turn their lives around.

45

3. **Hit Them Emotionally** – When you create your ad, you want to appeal to their emotions and not tell them only about the features of the property.

   What Not to Say – This home comes with a finished basement.

   What to Say – This professionally finished Rec Room is a fantastic added feature to this home. This basement is perfect for entertaining your family and friends or ideal for your in-home movie theatre.

4. **Get More Information for Free** – The best way to get people to call you is to get a 1-800 number where they can get additional information on the Rent to Own property you currently have listed and to leave a message to arrange a viewing of your home.

You have less than a second to grab their attention. You want them to call you and not your competitors. Here's an example of an ad that we have used successfully in the past.

Beautiful 3 Bedroom Rent to Own Home – Move in Ready

All Credit Scores Welcomed

For a video walkthrough of this beautiful home please visit

Video - **http://youtube/xxxXXXxxxXX**

We have a beautiful 3 bedroom, 3 bathroom **Rent to Own** home on a premium lot situated on a child friendly street. This home is located in a highly sought after north Whitby neighbourhood, close to all amenities including Walmart, Tim Horton's, Super-Store, LCBO, Beer Store, Bank Of Montreal, TD Bank, Scotia Bank, restaurants and much more.

As soon as you walk in you'll feel at home with a very spacious open concept on the main floor. The large master bedroom comes with a walk-in closet and a very convenient 4 piece en-suite bathroom with a separate shower and a beautiful oval tub to soak in after a hard day's work.

The professionally finished Rec Room is a fantastic added feature to this home. This basement is perfect for entertaining your family and friends or ideal for an in-home movie theatre. This home also comes with a beautifully landscaped backyard for you, your family and friends to enjoy for years to come.

Please call our free 24 hour message 7 days a week at **1-800-123-4567** for additional information or to schedule a walkthrough.

Using a video walkthrough can be good or bad.

Good in the sense that the people coming out to your home have had a chance to view your home and have a better idea of what it looks like, so will therefore be more interested.

Bad in the sense that you may not get as much traffic flowing to your property as you had hoped. You will however, get solid leads out to your properties that are very serious about moving into your home.

This is something I'll leave up to you to experiment with to see if it works for you.

Now, when you're making your videos, they don't have to be professional. Just be yourself; people want to know who you are. Please feel free to view some of our videos at:

http://smarthomechoice.ca

I have made some mistakes in a number of my videos, but I just left them in. I've had toilet seats left up, tried to open sliding doors that were jammed, etc. Have fun with it and be yourself.

Where to Advertise

Online

There are a number of free advertising sites on the Internet that you can use to get your phone to ring. The most popular free sites at the time of writing this are Kijiji™ and Craigslist™.

Your local area websites may not generate as many leads but I highly recommend that you get your ad onto as many sites as possible. Even if you only get 1 lead a week on a site that receives minimal traffic, it is better than none. You never know, that may be the person who will be perfect for your home. It may take a bit more of your time but it's worth it.

Remember that the websites below are being quoted at the time of the writing of this guide and are focused on reaching tenants within the province of Ontario.

www.kijiji.ca – Free (good traffic)
www.craigslist.ca – Free (good traffic)
www.isell.com – Free (limited traffic)
www.rentboard.ca – Paid advertising (good traffic)
www.viewit.ca – Paid advertising (good traffic)
www.gottarent.com – Paid advertising (good traffic)

When using **gottarent.com**™ your listing(s) will also appear on gscrentals.com, 247apartments.com, apartmentcorner.com, 101apartments.com, and actualhomes.com. Combined, these websites serve over 400,000 renters during the off-season months and over 550,000 renters during the peak months.

These are just a few sites that I've found that have provided us with great success. I'm sure there are many more out there, so take the time to do your own search to find other sites on which to advertise your property.

When you advertise your home, make sure to place the ad in the **House Rental** section and not the **For Sale** section. When I placed my ad in the For Sale section, I received very little response.

Another thing I found to be interesting was *when* I placed my ads. Monday morning at 8:00 am was a very active time period as well as lunch time (12:00 pm).

It may be different in your area, but either way, pay attention to your call volumes and determine the times throughout the week when you consistently experience higher than normal call volumes. This will be the time you want to bump up your ads to the front page.

Offline

This is a major area that so many people forget to take advantage of. This may be more important than advertising online. Many families that are looking to move into a particular area will drive around in that location to try to find a home for rent or sale.

> If you have a lawn sign or directional signs advertising your home, the leads that are generated from this are golden.

They are most likely familiar with the area, have family in the area and their kids go to school in the vicinity. Don't forget this stream of advertising.

Here is an example of a lawn and directional signs that I have used to generate leads to my homes. To help generate additional leads, I would also add directional arrows to your street signs to point them in the right direction of your home.

There are many companies out there that can produce these types of signs for you.

Make sure that the sign is generic so that you can use it for other properties you acquire in the future.

By Phone

Take a close look at the sign. Do you see the number that we used? I didn't use my own personal cell or home phone number; I used a 1-800 number.

Do not forget your 1-800 number. This allows you to have your future tenants call you, listen to a brief description of your property and allow you to set a scheduled time to call everyone back.

Most importantly, it allows you to have your family time and not be disturbed at all hours of the day/night.

> Family time is important. Do not have your personal
> cell phone ringing off the hook all day long.

I had calls coming in anywhere between 6:00 am to 12:00 am at night. It's important to control your rental properties and more importantly your time.

I'm sure there are many companies out there that provide 1-800 number services. The one we use is **eVoice**™.

http://www.evoice.com/

Up to this point, I have provided you with a number of different services to use. In no way am I promoting any company (honestly, I am not getting paid by them), I am simply providing you with resources that have worked for me.

If you find other companies that work for you, great! I would love to hear about them as they may be better than what I am using and can be shared with other investors.

On the next page is a sample script I have used that has worked very effectively for me over the past number of years.

1-800 Number Script

Thank you for calling about our Rent to Own program.

If you have a dream of becoming a homeowner, we can assist. The home that you are calling about is not only beautiful but is located in a wonderful, child friendly neighbourhood.

If you think that you have to save for a few more years to purchase your dream home, we have great news for you.

This program allows you to move into this beautiful home today, not years from now. The process is accomplished through a reasonable down payment at affordable monthly payments.

No bank financing is required and credit issues are not a problem.

You receive all the benefits of home ownership now and not 3 to 5 years from now!

No matter your situation: *newly divorced, past or present financial problems, self-employed, new immigrant to Canada or a single parent...*

Your credit can be good, bad or ugly; we don't care.

Please leave a brief message to schedule a walkthrough of this home and someone will call you back shortly
Thank you.

This pre-recorded message is like a sales robot for you that works 24 hours a day 7 days a week and never gets tired.

I don't put the address of my property in any of my advertisements. I want them to call me and I want them to get excited about the possibility of home ownership.

I also don't include the buyout price in my script. You don't want to scare people off before they even get a chance to view your home.

Step #5 – Booking Appointments and Tracking Calls

Now for the fun part... You get to talk to your first client!

Keep it simple!

Don't try to sell your home over the phone. I've tried this approach as have many other successful investors. It just doesn't work. Many times, you end up talking the other person on the other end of the line out of viewing your home.

Don't get caught up in trying to explain credits and buyout price. Spend the least amount of time possible on the phone with each person you talk to. The goal is to get them out to the home and to get them emotionally attached to the property. You don't need to sell the home, the home will sell itself.

There are times when someone will ask you lots of questions and want to know more about your program.

"I don't have the numbers with me, my wife or partner has them."

"I'm on my way to an appointment, but I can answer all your questions when you get to the property."

"Why don't you view the property first to see if you like the home and the neighbourhood?"

Trust me. I've talked so many prospects out of coming to my home because I thought I could sell them the property by explaining the program over the phone. It can be confusing trying to talk about credits, buyout price, where the credits go, how you come up with the numbers, etc.

> Make your home do the selling for you.
> Your job is to get them out to the property.

Common Questions

Although the goal is to spend the least amount of time on the phone, I'm not saying that you need to hang up on them or to be rude to cut the call short. You will encounter people who will not want to go to your property until they have a basic understanding of how the program works.

Here are the most common questions I get and the best way I have found to respond to them.

This applies to calls as well as emails.

How does it work?

Here's how it works, (name of tenant). The process works similar to leasing a car. Our program offers families that have some money to

> The best way to tackle this is to play
> good cop bad cop.

put down a chance to move into their home today without having to qualify for a mortgage. In addition, a portion of your monthly rent and your initial down payment goes towards the purchase of the home. Our program has helped future homeowners save close to $15,000 in a 3 year lease that is then used towards the purchase of their home.

Are utilities included?

Thanks for your inquiry. As this is a Rent to Own program, our goal is to prepare you for home ownership. As you are not responsible for paying taxes or insurance, the utilities would be your responsibility. We will be at the property this Wednesday at 7:00 pm. Please confirm if you would like to view this property.

I'm in a bankruptcy/consumer proposal, can you help?

Fortunately, your bankruptcy situation may be something we can assist you with. We've helped a number of families in this scenario by working closely with them and our lending specialist to fix any credit issues.

In order for us to better assist you, it would be best if we were able to meet to go through your situation in greater detail.

I have a showing at one of our properties this Wednesday at 7:00 pm. It's located at xxxxxxx and I believe it would be beneficial for you to come and view it.

How to Book Your Appointments

When you are booking appointments for people to view your home, do not set individual appointments for every call. The best way to do this is to have them all come at the same time. By doing this, you create an auction like environment that creates a demand for your home.

It's also a great idea to show your property at least twice a week. I prefer an evening showing and a day showing on the weekend. By doing this you accommodate almost everyone's schedule who may be interested in viewing your property.

I avoid telling them that it's an Open House, but rather describe it as an appointment. If you tell them it's an Open House, most times they will think it's optional and may not come.

Before you hang up, make sure you ask this important question. If you are unable to make your appointment, can you please call me to cancel?

Let them reply. Don't make it a statement, it's important to phrase it as a question. By doing this, it drastically decreases the amount of no shows.

> Another way to increase your turn out to your
> properties is to smile through the phone.

As simple as that sounds, it works, trust me! I didn't believe it until I started to do it and my turn out rates went through the roof. The person on the other end of the line can hear you smile. So before you call someone back put your fun hat on and smile!

Another important thing to do is to track each call that comes in. By tracking the calls, you can write down some information on each person coming to your home on the day of the viewing.

I like to take it one step further and do follow-up calls the day of to ensure they are still coming. It's not necessary to do this since you've already asked them to call you should they have to cancel. However, it's just a final fail proof step that we prefer to take.

There are two ways to track your calls. Both work effectively and it's entirely up to you how you prefer to do it.

The Spreadsheet

This is a copy of the spreadsheet I use to track each of my calls.

LEAD TRACKER - SMART HOME CHOICE

NAME	PHONE	CON	EMAIL	NOTES

Calendar Entry in Cell Phone

The second way of tracking your calls and setting appointments is to add a calendar entry into your cell phone with your lead's phone number.

I'll add their names, time of their appointment and some brief notes. The good thing about doing it this way is that no matter where I am I can give them a call to remind them with just a few clicks on my phone.

Again, each way is effective. It really comes down to your preference.

Step # 6 Preparation for the Big Day

Before you head out to your property, the most important thing is to make sure you have all your documentation ready to go. The last thing you want is **NOT** to have any applications forms or fact sheets at the property. Trust me... I've been there and it is not a good place to be.

On the next page are all the things you need to make sure you have before you get out to the property.

Sign-in Sheet

Here's a copy of the sign-in sheet that I use to track everyone that comes out to my properties.

Sign In Sheet - Smart Home Choice				
NAME	**PHONE#**	**EMAIL**	**DOWNPAYMENT**	**HOW DID YOU FIND US?**

For the sign-in sheet, I will usually have a name at the top with all the required spots filled in, especially the down payment. I like using $5,000 as it sets a good standard for the type of down payment I am looking for. If you have a beautiful home that is in a great location, try using $10,000. I have had success with using both types of down payments.

By doing this, I have discovered that the first person that shows up and fills in your sign-in sheet will also fill out each section and then everyone else will as well.

> If you leave your sign-in sheet blank, almost all of your tenants that sign-in will also leave certain areas blank.

The sign-in sheet is important as it allows you to follow up with everyone that has visited the property and to walk them through the next steps if they are serious candidates.

Fast Approval Application Form

The next thing that you want to make sure that you have is probably one of the most important things - the application form. Imagine having someone interested in your property after you have explained to them how the program works, but you have no application forms.

If tenants see that you are unorganized, they will quickly lose interest and move to another property.

> Always be prepared. It is the most important thing you can do when you have a vacant property.

On the next page is a copy of the application form that we give our future homeowners to fill out.

FAST Approval Form
Rent to Own Application

Anyone over the age of 18 must complete a separate approval form
PLEASE PRINT - ALL information must be completed.
1-888-123-4567 Fax
Full Name _____
E-Mail Address_____
Home Phone (_____)_____
Cell Phone (___)_____
Social Insurance Number _____-_____-_____
Date of Birth _____
Present Address _____
_____City_____
Province _____ Postal Code _____
How long at current address? _____
Current Rent/Payment $ _____
Landlord/mgr's name _____ Phone (_____)_____ _____
Employer_____
Position _____ How Long?_____
Home Phone (_____)_____
Phone (___)_____
Name and relationship of everyone living with you
_____
Any pets? Describe _____
Yearly income before deductions (include all income sources) $_____
When would you like to move in? _____
How much of a down payment can you raise? _____
Which savings program do you prefer? (Circle one) '
Regular Savings' 'Super Savings'

Is your credit, good, fair, or ugly? _____
I declare that the application is complete, true and correct and I herewith give my permission for anyone contacted (including TransUnion or Equifax) to release the credit or personal information of the undersigned applicant to Management or their authorized agents, at any time, for the purposes of entering into and continuing to offer or collect on any agreement and/or credit extended. I further authorize Management or their Authorized Agents to verify the application information including but not limited to obtaining criminal records, contacting creditors, present or former landlords, employers and personal references, whether listed or not, at the time of the application and at any time in the future, with regard to any agreement entered into with Management. Any false information will constitute grounds for rejection of this application, or Management may at any time immediately terminate any agreement entered into in reliance upon misinformation given on the application. By providing the home phone numbers and e-mail addresses above, I/we hereby authorize the Vendor to contact me/us at my/our home phone numbers or e-mail addresses.

_____
Applicant's Name (Print)
_____
Signature & Date

63

Map of Schools

One of the many questions I get when I'm at the property is "are there any schools nearby?"

Half of the time I have no idea. So the best way to tackle this is to go to Google Maps™ and type in the address of your rental property. Once you've completed this, type in schools and all the schools in the vicinity will populate close to your rental property. Print off a few copies and have them at the home. You will look like a genius.

Deposit Receipt

Deposit receipts are another important thing to have at your property. I'm sure you are tired of me saying that everything is important, but it is.
If someone is in love with your property, a great way to get a commitment from them is to have them leave a deposit. By doing this, they now have a vested interest in the home and have proved to you that they are serious.

On the next page is the Deposit Receipt Sheet.

DEPOSIT RECEIPT TO HOLD PROPERTY

_____ (Prospective Tenant) is agreeing to a deposit of $_____ paid to hold Prospective Tenant's position for the property located at: _____ _____, Ontario.

This complete deposit shall be paid as follows: $_____ on _____,_____ and the remaining $_____ will be paid on _____,_____. All of Prospective Tenant's deposit will apply towards the purchase of said property (it will be considered as part of Prospective Tenant's Option Payment) provided Prospective Tenant lives up to all other terms of his/her/their agreement with Landlord. This deposit is non-refundable, and Prospective Tenant must pay additional $_____ option consideration by _____ and his/her/their first and last month's rent of $ _____ before moving into the property on _____. If either of these payments is not received by Landlord on time then Landlord may at Landlord's sole discretion cancel agreement with Prospective Tenant and all money paid to Landlord by Prospective tenant shall be kept as liquidated damages to cover application review, marketing costs to fill property, and lost opportunities. This agreement is subject to Landlord's final approval of Prospective Tenant's application. In the event that Landlord does not approve for any reason, Landlord may at his/her sole discretion refund all of Prospective Tenant's deposit and cancel this agreement. All option payments and first month's rent must be in the form of either certified funds or money order except for noted below.

Prospective Tenant understands that Prospective Tenant does NOT have a valid lease or option to purchase said property UNTIL Prospective Tenant makes all payments described above on time and signs all further paperwork with Landlord, including Lease Agreement, Option to Purchase Agreement, any Disclosure Forms, etc. In no case may the Prospective Tenant enter or otherwise occupy said property until ALL conditions and terms in this agreement have been fulfilled. TIME IS OF THE ESSENCE!

_____ _____/_____/_____

Prospective Tenant

_____ _____/_____/_____

Landlord and/ Agent for Landlord

If initial deposit is to be paid by cheque, initial next to this paragraph to show both parties understand and agree to the following: Tenant understands the he/she/they are making a non refundable deposit on this date to hold property. Furthermore, Tenant hereby states that there are sufficient funds available to cover this cheque and that Tenant understands Landlord is relying upon the fact that this cheque will in fact clear. In the event this cheque does not clear for any reason, Tenant understands that Tenant shall be liable for prosecution and collection to the fullest extent of the law. Furthermore, Tenant understands that all remaining option money and first month's rent must be in the form of either certified funds or money order.

65

You may have several people that are interested in your property. If that's the case you can take more than one deposit however, if you decide on one family over the next, the right thing to do is to return anyone's deposit that you did not accept.

If the family that you select changes their mind, the agreement stipulates that it's non-refundable. Why?

Let's say that you have done a credit check, gone through the entire approval process of reviewing their pay stub, tax assessment, bank statements, etc.. This is time consuming and you should be compensated for the amount of work you have done.

While we are on this point, NEVER take your property off the market and NEVER stop showing your home until you have a signed agreement and a substantial amount of money received for your Rent to Own property.

I've seen it happen to investors time and time again. They will stop advertising, 3 to 4 weeks go by, and the tenant decides to back out.

Guess what? You now have to advertise your home all over again. How do I know this? I've made the same mistake.

Required Information

The next thing that I like to have at the property is a document outlining all the required information that is needed to verify their income that will allow them to move into the property.

Offering them this hand-out sheet after they have filled in an application provides clarity about everything else that is required.

Here is what I use.

Future Homeowner Checklist

Next Steps: Please complete and fax to 1-888-123-4567 or scan and send to info@smarthomechoice.ca

Please allow 2 to 3 business days to complete once all the required information below has been received. Once you are approved, one of our associates will be in contact with you to walk you through the next steps into home ownership.

- 2 years tax assessments
- Recent pay stub **and** 3 months of bank statements (where current rent/mortgage payments are coming from)
- Other sources of income
- Driver's license (photocopy front and back)
- Proof of down payment amount (screenshot of account / copy of statement)

Key Features and Benefits for the Tenant/Future Homeowner

Maximum Leverage: You are spending very little money to control a very expensive, and very profitable, piece of real estate.

Time: Before you actually buy the home, you will have 12-36 months (depending on your agreement) to repair your credit, find the best interest rates, investigate the home, and research the neighbourhood and/or schools.

Rent Money is Working Toward the Purchase of the Home: Every month a portion of your rent payment (typically $200-$400, depending on the program) is credited towards your down payment.

Credit Problems are Okay: Qualification restrictions simply do not exist. You will be approved at the sole discretion of the seller.

No Lengthy Mortgage Approvals: Your approval will be based solely at the discretion of the seller instead of a lender who can take up to a month (or longer) to render a decision.

Control of the Home: You will be put in full legal control of the home for a specified period of time without actually having to own it.

Be Familiar with the Benefits of Rent to Own Before You Get to the Property

Before going out to your property to show it for the first time, make sure you are familiar with the benefits of Rent to Own. This will help you answer any questions that come up. Here is a list of 27 benefits of Rent to Own.

Financial Benefits

1. **Rent Money is working Toward the Purchase of the Home:** Every month a portion of your rent payment (typically $200-$400, depending on the program) is credited towards your down payment.
2. **Down Payment towards the Purchase of the Home:** When you sign a Rent to Own contract, you will pay the seller an option deposit (down payment). This money is your vested interest in the home and will be fully (100%) credited to you when you buy the home.
3. **Minimum Cash Out of Pocket:** When you purchase a home conventionally, you must pay at least 5% down plus closing costs. When you buy with a Lease to Purchase, you pay first and last month's rent and a small option deposit.
4. **Profits from Appreciation:** Since the sales price is locked in before closing (as specified in your agreement), any increase in property value will mean that your equity (what you owe minus what it's worth) is increasing in the home.
5. **Credit Problems are Okay:** Qualification restrictions simply do not exist. You will be approved at the sole discretion of the seller.
6. **Clean Up Your Credit Issues:** Re-establishing your credit with a mortgage specialist will allow you to attain the lowest interest rate at the end of the term.
7. **No Lengthy Mortgage Approvals:** Your approval will be based solely on the discretion of the seller instead of a lender who can take up to a month (or longer) to render a decision.

8. **No Taxes, Less Liability:** Since you do not own the home (yet), you will not have to pay property taxes and your liability exposure will be dramatically reduced.
9. **Maximum Leverage:** You are spending very little money to control a very expensive, and very profitable, piece of real estate.
10. **Customized Terms:** You get to select the payment amount that you are comfortable with and purchase the home anytime during your agreed upon term.
11. **Know your Purchase Price:** Knowing what your purchase price is provides transparency and a benchmark for all of your credit needs to successfully secure a mortgage on your home.
12. **Fixed Monthly Payments:** This helps you budget your finances on a month-to-month basis.
13. **No Rent Increases for 3 years:** If you are a renter, your landlord usually raises the rent each year. The rise in rental amount can be anywhere from $25 to hundreds of dollars, depending on your area.
14. **Save Enough Down Payment:** Insufficient down payment is not an issue with a Rent to Own property. Our program will ensure that you have enough saved at the end of your term in order to purchase the home that you're in.
15. **Free Property Inspection:** In many cases the home has already been inspected saving you $300 to $500 dollars. I ensure the property is professionally inspected prior to you moving in.
16. **Forced Savings:** Our program allows you to save money from a portion of your rent while you are in your home. This planning makes saving for your home possible and easy.

Personal Benefits

1. **Control of the Home:** You will be put in full legal control of the home for a specified period of time without actually having to own it.

2. **Quick Move in Time:** You can typically take possession of the home in less than 1 week instead of conventional move in times of 1 to 3 months after your offer was accepted.
3. **Time:** Before you actually buy the home, you will have 12-36 months (depending on your agreement) to repair your credit, find the best interest rates, investigate the home, and research the neighbourhood and/or schools
4. **Minimal Maintenance:** Large maintenance problems or any maintenance problems that exceed a certain amount of money are delegated to the seller.
5. **Customize Your Living Space:** Feel free to add a patio in the backyard, finish your basement, paint, etc.
6. **Freedom of Your Choice:** We are obligated by law to sell you the property however you have the liberty to decide in the end.
7. **No Surprises or Fine Print:** Everything is explained up front and there are no hidden costs.
8. **Your Opportunity to Experience Home Ownership:** If you've owned your own home in the past you'll understand what we mean. Enjoy the feeling of being in control of your own living space. No need to fear that your landlord has to sell the house.
9. **Do Your Laundry in Your Own House:** Most apartments and some rental houses don't have a washing machine and dryer in the unit or home. You may have to walk down a hall, a flight of stairs, or walk or drive to a laundromat to get your washing done. Just think of the extra time you will be gaining each week while doing your laundry in your own house.
10. **Create a More Stable Life for Your Kids:** Each year you live in your house, you are creating roots to your community. Your kids will grow up with the same friends at school and you will eventually know many other people in the area as well.
11. **Choose your home:** If you're interested in choosing your own home, we can help. We will advise you on the proper locations to choose from.

A short list of all the things required at the property

- Clipboard for your sign-in sheet
- Pens
- Table and chairs for your presentation
- Calculator
- Fast Approval Application
- Sign-in Sheet
- Client Checklist
- Deposit Receipt
- Yard Sign
- Lockbox
- Map of school locations in the area
- Savings Program
- Toilet paper
- Air freshener
- Light bulbs

Remember, whatever you do... do not stop advertising until you have a substantial amount of money received and the agreements have been signed.

Step #7 Show Time – Smile

This is the moment you've been waiting for. This is the time to be yourself and have fun with what you've done up to this point. The best tip I can give you is to be yourself and to be truthful.

Believing in what you are doing is a truly good thing. You are helping individuals or families into home ownership and are sincerely trying to turn their lives around by helping them to find a fresh start.

Arrive at your property at least 20 minutes before your first appointment to ensure all the lights are turned on to help brighten up the home. If you are doing a day showing, make sure all the blinds are opened to let in as much sunlight as possible. If it's cold outside, crank up the heat and if it is hot outside turn on the A/C to cool the place down. Put some air fresheners in the house to keep the property smelling clean. Also, if you have a gas fireplace, light it.

The key is to showcase your home and to make it look its BEST!!

DING DONG!

When they come to the door, introduce yourself and have them sign in. As mentioned earlier, this is incredibly important for tracking who came to the property and who didn't. Make sure that you get their e-mail address and phone numbers. You also want to make sure that their writing is legible so that if you need to follow up with them, you can.

> Your sign-in sheet is GOLD, make sure you can
> read it and it is legible!

Once they have signed-in, have them walk through the property on their own and let them know that once they've completed their tour that you will be available to answer any questions they may have.

If you have a busy open house, these are the two different things that will happen:

1. They don't like the house and will leave. I have no issues with this as no one is wasting anyone's time. They simply do not like your home. This doesn't mean that you have an ugly home; it just means that it doesn't work for them and their family.
2. They love the home and require additional information. If they love it, they will wait around to discuss the details of the home even if you are busy with another client.

If they like the home and come back to you with additional questions, explain how the program works and be sincere.

There are a number of different ways to explain how the program works. Below are key points to remember to say and not to say when explaining your fact sheet.

Remember, the fact sheet can only do so much. It's up to you to sell the home and to sell them the dream of how close they are to home ownership.

Do

- Explain that although they are paying more each month, they are paying less than market rent as a portion is automatically going towards the down payment.
- Show them the benefit of being in the higher rent bracket as the credits earned are doubled.
- Let them know that they are able to paint and decorate the home. I also let them know that they can complete the basement and remove carpeting for hardwood flooring just as long as it is professionally done and I'm notified of any major renovations.
- Explain to them how Rent to Own is much better than renting as their hard earned money is not all going towards the landlord.
- Let them know that you are looking for a family who is serious about getting into home ownership and who will look after your property. Generally, you will notice that the family who has the largest down payment does exactly that.
- Purchase of the home is not an obligation; it's an option at the end of the term.
- Be honest and truthful. If they ask you how you came up with your buyout price, tell them the truth.

Don't

The only major don't is:

Never say how much of a down payment is required first!

This is incredibly important. If you tell them how much of a down payment you require, you could potentially be leaving thousands of dollars on the table. Explain to them that the larger the down payment, the better their chances are of getting into the home.

If their offer is lower than what you are looking for, it's always easier to try to increase their deposit if they say a number first.

Typical Questions You Will Get at Your Open House

Below are some typical questions we get asked during our Open Houses.

What is a Rent to Own Home?

A Rent to Own home is a home that you lease, but you also control the property by having the option to purchase it during your lease period. We cannot market the home for sale, since we are bound by an agreement to sell the home to you at a pre-determined price, agreed on before you move in.

Who pays the property taxes and insurance during the Rent to Own?

The homeowner pays the property taxes and insurance.

I am renting now, how is this different?

This is the best way to help you get started towards BUYING your own home. Part of your rent payment goes towards your home. This is a much better option instead of throwing your money away each month on rent and having nothing to show for it at the end of the year. In addition, your rent stays the same for the duration of your term.

My credit is less than perfect, can you still help me?

Yes, in many cases we can. The Rent to Own program was specifically designed to help families with blemished credit, or those who are self-employed or lacking the required down payment. Qualifications for Rent to Own homes are based on your ability to make the monthly payments, not on the strength of your credit score. You get to stay in the home you want while your credit score is improving.

Can I have my lawyer look at the paperwork?

Absolutely, we prefer you have legal representation look over the paperwork however, if you choose not to, that is fine as well.

Can I renovate my home?

Yes, as long as the homeowner is contacted and agrees prior to any major changes and the work is performed by a qualified tradesperson. Apart from that we have no problem with it as you are improving the value of your home.

How much credit is given for each monthly payment?

It depends on the Rent to Own program. Each program is custom designed for the Rent to Own buyer. Credits typically range from $200 to $400 per month.

Who pays for utilities (heat, hydro and water)?

In the Rent to Own program, you are responsible for paying heat, hydro, water and any other utilities associated with the property including phone, cable and internet.

What happens if I can't qualify with a lender at the end of the program?

At the end of the Rent to Own program, if you cannot qualify with a lender, the program can be adjusted and reviewed until you are ready to purchase the home.

Who pays for repairs?

As a future homeowner, you have to experience all aspects of home ownership, including repairs. You are responsible for any minor repairs however larger issues that exceed $500 such as heating, roof, etc. will be the homeowners' responsibility.

What do I have to sign?

A standard Lease Agreement and an Option to Purchase Agreement.

What's required prior to me moving in?

What we normally look for is a recent tax assessment, recent pay-stub, three months of bank statements, a photocopy of your drivers license, and a completed fast approval form for anyone moving in over the age of 18.

How long is the program?

The typical Rent to Own program is a 3 year term. This gives our credit specialist time to help you restore your credit and this will also lock in your rent price for 3 years without fluctuation.

How do you choose the price at the end of the term?

We use an average appreciation value based on historic market values in the area the house is located to calculate the Future Purchase Price.

Who pays the insurance on the home?

The owner is responsible for paying for the building insurance on the home until you are ready to purchase. However, you and your family will require contents/tenant insurance which covers items inside your home including personal belongings.

What if I decide not to exercise my option to purchase?

In extreme cases, if you decide not to exercise your option to purchase you will lose your initial deposit and monthly option premiums which can add up to thousands of dollars. We always recommend that you purchase the home and then sell if you have outgrown it or need to move due to job relocation, etc.

After you have explained the process and your prospective tenant is excited about moving into your home and you have answered all their questions, this is the next important step.

Application Form

Have them fill out a Fast Approval Application. Don't give them a chance to fax it in or e-mail it. Have them fill it out at your property. If they leave with the application, you will never see them or your application again. Let them know that you have many families interested in the property and that you would like to make a decision within the next day or 2.

Anyone that is going to be living in the home over the age of 18 should fill out a Fast Approval Application. The reason this is important is that if the rent isn't paid, you can file with the tenant board for each individual if required. Let's hope that never happens, but it's better to protect yourself than NOT.

Once the application has been completed, make sure you go through it while they are there. Make sure it's legible and that everything has been properly filled out. You would hate for them to leave and find out that you can't contact them because you can't make out their phone number.

Also, make sure that the application is signed. This allows you to do a credit check. Now some people may say, "what's the point of a credit check, if you know it's no good anyway?"

That's true, but you want to see their history. Did they just have a bad stretch and need your assistance to get back on their feet? Do they have a long history of slow payments or never paying anything back?

I highly recommend the credit check. It is money well spent!

Deposit

Don't be shy to ask them for a deposit. If they are truly serious about this property, they can leave a deposit and you will issue a receipt to them.

Most families will give anywhere from $100 to several hundred dollars for an initial deposit. By doing this, it shows that you have a very serious candidate who is interested in moving into your home.

Remember, let them know that their deposit will be part of their down payment and it is fully refundable if they are not selected.

Future Homeowner Checklist

Before they leave, make sure you explain to them the additional required information you will need. This is when I will give them a copy of the "Future Homeowner Checklist". It has all the information I'm looking for before I allow them to move into my property.

Refer to Chapter 6 for the Checklist.

If they are seriously interested in the property and are organized, they will have no issues gathering this information.

Don't hesitate to ask, "When can I expect to receive the required documentation in order to complete the approval process?"

You want to get a confirmed deadline from them. You don't want to make the mistake of waiting too long. If you do, they may find another home that catches their interest and you have now lost a prime candidate.

> Time is of the essence, so act fast. Let them know that you will be making a decision later that day or the next morning.

Also, for any applications that you fill out, make notes on the back. The next day, you don't want to be racking your brains about each tenant that filled out an application. Do it while it's fresh in your head.

By doing this, it will help you narrow down the tenants suitable for your home and you don't have to start running credit checks on families that end up wasting your time and efforts.

It's also important not to run credit checks until you have received all of the required information and have determined that they can afford your home.

The Largest Down Payment on the Home Wins!

The larger their down payment, the more they have at stake and are serious about getting into home ownership. The larger their down payment, the better their chances are of getting a mortgage at the end of the term.

Now, you may run into a situation where you have a family that loves the Rent to Own program however, the property you have may not be in the right location or the right size for their family. What I normally do is let them know that I can allow them to go out and select the home of their choice if they have a large enough down payment that makes it reasonable for me to do this.

Do **NOT** offer this solution unless you know for sure the home you have will not suit their needs.

Do **NOT** offer this in front of other families. The last thing you want is for 5 families in your home to know that you offer this solution and now you can't fill your home.

So you have two options, make note and call them back the next day or have them fill out an application and a Future Homeowner Profile Sheet. Take a look at the example on the next page.

VIP Client - Future Homeowner Profile

Name (s):_____

Phone (cell):_____

(home):_____

(E-mail):_____

- Preferred amount bedrooms _____
- Preferred amount bathrooms: _____
- Preferred square footage of home: _____
- Preferred location
  - 1_____
  - 2_____
  - 3 _____
- Type of home (circle): townhouse   semi-detached detached   other _____
- Family members _____
- Down payment amount: $ 10,000 (preferred) other:_____
- Afford monthly: $_____
- Lease end date for current place of residence: _____
- How many cars: _____
- When are you looking to move in: _____
- 2 Priority items for your home: _____ _____
- Credit (circle):   Good   Fair   Poor

Now if you are not in the position to purchase another home right away for the future homeowners, no problem. Let us know and we can assist with your deal.

After your Open House has completed, make sure you give your partner who helped you with the Open House a high five, or a huge pat on your own back if you did it all on your own.

The more Open Houses you host, the better you will be at them. It is amazing how well intuition guides you in making the right decision. Listen to it, it never lies.

Perhaps one day we may be calling on you for your services to help us fill one of our vacant properties.

Step #8 – The Next Day

Before you make your call, here is an important lesson I was once taught. Before you pick up the phone, determine if it is minor or major. If it is a minor call, such as calling a friend or family member to say hi, enjoy the call. If it is major, write down all your points and have an agenda prepared.

It is as equally important the next day to smile through the phone as it was when you initially called your potential client to show them your home.

Call back all of your potential tenants to find out their thoughts on the home and when will they have the required information and down payment available.

It is important to act quickly while the home is still fresh in their minds and their emotions are high. Once you have located a suitable tenant for your home, there are number of important steps to follow.

Gathering All Their Information

Anytime we are selecting a candidate for our home, we always want to see the following:

- 2 years tax assessments
- Recent pay stub **and** 3 months of bank statements (where current rent/mortgage payments are coming from)
- Other sources of income (pension, child support or alimony)
- Driver's licence (photocopy front and back)

Tax Assessment

The Tax Assessment also referred to as the Notice of Assessment, shows that they are paying their taxes on time. Now, if they are self-employed it may not be the best source to show what their true income is but it is a start.

Pay Stub

A recent pay stub is proof that they are gainfully employed and that they have regular income. If they are self-employed, we will ask to see their invoices over a 3 month term. This helps to determine what they can afford on a monthly basis.

Bank Statements

What we really like to see is a potential tenant's bank account statement, so that we know when their rent is being paid and where their cheques are being deposited. If they have multiple accounts and their rent is coming out of one account and their pay cheque is going into another, we prefer to see both.

This ensures that they are earning money from their current job and they are paying their rent or mortgage on time. This is also important information because it allows us to see what their current rent/mortgage is as well as other expenses and obligations they have on a monthly basis.

For example, if they are currently paying $700 in rent, and they are looking to move up to $1,800 a month in rent, you want to make sure they have the ability to pay you.

Many people will call their landlords. You can do that, but I usually do not. The reason is because if they are tenants that never pay on time, or maybe ever and their landlord wants them out, why would the landlord tell you the truth?

If the landlord desperately wants them out of their home, they will say whatever is needed to dump this unwanted baggage on you.

Other Sources of Income

By providing bank statements you will see if they have any other sources of income coming in such as baby bonuses, child support, GST cheques, etc.

This helps with the calculations and you will know whether or not they can afford your property.

Driver's Licence

The last thing to verify is their driver's licence. This is for identification purposes to ensure they are who they say they are.

Formula

To determine if the tenant can afford your property, try using this formula below:

Say for example your prospective tenants are making a combined income of $65,000 a year. It is recommended that their rent is less than one third of their gross monthly salary.

Here is the formula to use:
$$\$65,000 / 12 / 3 = \$1,805$$
Based on this calculation, you would not want them paying any more than $1,800 a month on rent, not including utilities.

By using this formula, I continue to have a high percentage of success with each of our tenants and properties that we own.

Some important questions to ask before moving forward...

While they were at the property, you may not have had an opportunity to ask them all the required information you needed to make your final decision. Something may have slipped your mind or you may have had a full house and did not want to ask any personal questions for others to hear.

Here are a few important questions to make sure you ask:

- How many people will be moving in with you?
- Do you have any pets?
- How many vehicles?
- Current rent payment?
- Why are you moving?
- How soon are you looking to move in?
- Have you had any bankruptcy or consumer proposals?
- How long have you been at your current job?

One of the most frequently asked questions we get is, ``should I allow pets?``

This entirely up to you... but we do.

The reason we do is because we have properly screened the tenants. They are putting down a substantial deposit before they move in meaning there is an incentive for them to own the home. We have a few properties today with pet owners and have had no issues at all.

The key is to frequently visit your property to make sure it is being properly maintained.

> Once you have collected all the required information, it is time to collect additional funds and sign the agreements.

The Next Meeting

Now there are 2 different options you have for arranging to collect the additional funds and signing the lease and option to purchase agreement:

- Meet at the property they will be moving into.
- Meet at their current place of residence.

By visiting where they currently live, you will have an opportunity to see how they live and to determine if they are tidy. Again, listen to your GUT! It's never wrong and it is there to protect you.

Do not be hasty in your decision making. When you do that you make wrong decisions and it can end up costing you thousands of dollars. If someone needs to move into your property in 2 or 3 days, this is usually a red flag.

Before you meet with the tenant that is going to be moving into your property, it is important that you familiarize yourself with the lease and option to purchase agreement.

Both agreements are attached for you to view. Just remember to have your lawyers review any forms before signing them.

LEASE AGREEMENT
Schedule A

THIS AGREEMENT, dated _____, 20__ is by and between_____, "Owners/Managers," and _____"Tenants," for rental of the dwelling located at **xxxxxxxxx, xxxxxxx, xxxxx** under the following terms and conditions:

FIXED-TERM AGREEMENT (LEASE) - Tenants agree to lease this dwelling for a fixed term of _____years, commencing on the ____ day of _____,20__, and ending on the ____ day of _____, 20__. Upon expiration, this Agreement shall become a month-to-month agreement AUTOMATICALLY, UNLESS either Tenants or Owners notify the other party in writing at least thirty (30) days prior to expiration that they do not wish this Agreement to continue on any basis. If the dwelling is not available for occupancy on the commencement date, Owner will not be responsible for any damages incurred by Tenants.

RENT – The rent shall be $_____ Dollars per month during the term of this lease, each for the first twelve (12) months and $_____ Dollars per month for months thirteen (13) through thirty–six (36). The Landlord acknowledges receipt from the Tenant of the sum of $_____Dollars as prepayment of the last month's rent.

In the event that Tenant remains in the home beyond thirty-six (36) months, the rent shall increase by 2.1% per annum. This rent increase will be due and payable at the lease anniversary date each year.

FORM OF PAYMENT - Tenants agree to pay rent in the form of a personal cheque, cashier's cheque, or a money order made out to Owners.

RENT PAYMENT PROCEDURE - Tenants agree to mail their rent to Owners at the following address:

_____.

PAYMENT WILL BE MADE VIA POSTDATED CHEQUES or in such a way as Owners advise the Tenants in writing.

RETURNED CHEQUES - If, for any reason, a cheque used by Tenants to pay Owners is returned without having been paid, Tenants will pay a returned cheque charge of forty-five dollars ($45) AND be responsible for any other damages incurred by Owner in connection therewith. After the second time that a Tenants' cheque is returned, Tenants must thereafter secure a cashier's cheque or money order for payment of rent.

_____

Tenant

_____

Owners/Managers

RENT DUE DATE; RENT LATE DATE - The due date for the rent owing under this Agreement, including, without limitation, late payment penalty, is the FIRST (1ST) day of every calendar month. The very next day is the rent late date. This is the first day when Owners will consider the rent late. Owners expect to have RECEIVED the rent before this date. If Tenants' rent is due on the first, it must be paid on or before the third (3rd) to be "on time."

UTILITIES/SERVICES – Tenants agree to pay all utilities with respect to the premises, including, without limitation, the following: utilities, gas, electric, water/sewer, cable TV, telephones and garbage removal if applicable.

OCCUPANTS - The number of occupants is limited to __. Only the following persons may live in this dwelling:_____,
_____,   _____,
_____, _____. No one else may live there, even temporarily, without Owner's prior written permission.

SUBLETTING AND ASSIGNMENT - Tenants shall not sublet the entire premises or any part of the premises, nor shall they assign this Agreement to anyone else without first obtaining Owners' written permission.

LIQUID-FILLED FURNITURE - Tenants agree not to keep any liquid-filled furniture in this dwelling without first obtaining Owners' written permission.

DAMAGE TO PERSONAL PROPERTY - All personal property belonging to Tenants or to any other person shall be kept in the leased premises at the sole risk of Tenants or such other person, and neither Owners nor Owners' agent, if any, shall be liable for the theft, misappropriation, damage or injury thereto, nor for damage or injury to Tenants or to other persons caused by water, snow, frost, steam, heat or cold, dampness, falling plaster, sewers or sewage, gas, odors, noise, flooding, bursting or leaking pipes, plumbing, electrical wiring and equipment and fixtures of all kinds, or for any act, negligence, or omission of other Tenants or occupants, if any, of the structure in which the leased premises are located; provided, however, nothing herein shall be deemed to be a waiver of Owners' responsibility for the negligence or willful acts of Owners, or Owners' agents and employees. Tenants shall indemnify, defend and hold Owners harmless from all costs, expenses, liability, claims, actions, causes of action, or damages sustained by reason of any occurrence causing injury or death to any person or damage to property due directly or indirectly to Tenants' acts or omissions or occupancy of the leased premises or those of its agents, employees or invitees.

_____
Tenant

_____
Owners/Managers

VEHICLES - Tenants agree to keep a maximum of ___ vehicles on the premises. These vehicles must be both operable and currently licensed. Tenants agree to park their vehicles in assigned spaces and to keep those spaces clean of oil drippings. Tenants agree to advise their visitors about parking and to take responsibility for where their visitors park. Only those motorcycles that have exhaust muffling comparable to that of a passenger car are allowed. Only those self-propelled recreational vehicles which are licensed and which are used for regular personal transportation are allowed. Tenants agree not to park boats, recreational trailers, utility trailers, and the like on the premises without first obtaining Owners' written permission. Tenants agree not to repair their vehicles on the premises if such repairs will take longer than a single day unless the vehicle is kept in an enclosed garage.

APPLIANCES - Although there may be appliances in the dwelling, such as a refrigerator, stove, dishwasher, freezer, dryer, garbage compactor, or air conditioner, the use of these appliances is not included in the rent. If Tenants wish to use these appliances, they agree to assume all responsibility for care and maintenance. Further, Tenants will return such appliances to Owners in the same condition as received, reasonable wear and tear excepted. If Tenants wish to use their own appliances, they may request that the Owners' appliances be removed from the premises.

TENANTS INSPECTION - Tenants have inspected the dwelling and its contents and agree that they are in satisfactory order, as are the electrical, plumbing, and heating systems. Tenants hereby accept the premises in their "AS IS," "WHERE IS" condition. The Owners are not making any representation or warranties regarding the condition or fitness of the premises.

NOTIFICATION OF SERIOUS BUILDING PROBLEMS - Tenants agree to notify the Owners immediately upon first discovering any signs of serious building problems such as a crack in the foundation, a tilting porch, a crack in the plaster or stucco, moisture in the ceiling, buckling sheetrock or siding, a leaky roof, a spongy floor, a leaky water heater, or termite activity. Tenants shall comply with the requirements imposed on Tenants by all applicable provincial and local housing, health and safety codes and/or by any insurer of the leased premises. Tenants shall not use the leased premises for any unlawful purpose and shall not in any way disturb or annoy any other neighbors.

MINOR REPAIRS - Tenants are responsible for the first five hundred dollars ($500) of repairs or replacements in any one-month. Owners are responsible for amounts above five hundred dollars ($500) in any one month. Furthermore, Tenants will return the premises to Owners in the same condition as received, reasonable wear and tear excepted.

_____
Tenant

_____
Owners/Managers

WINDOWS - Except for those windows which are noted in writing as being cracked or broken when Tenants move in, Tenants agree to be responsible for any windows which become cracked or broken in their dwelling while they live there and such costs shall not be taken into account with respect to the five hundred dollar ($500) threshold. Tenants may repair the windows themselves if they can do the work in a professional manner. Otherwise, they may hire a glazier or submit a maintenance request to Owners. If they submit a maintenance request, Owners will charge them no more for the work than the least expensive written bid for the work that Tenants can obtain from a professional glazier.

DRAIN STOPPAGES - As of the date of this Agreement, Owners warrant that the dwelling's sewage drains are in good working order and that they will accept the normal household waste for which they were designed. They will not accept things such as paper diapers, sanitary napkins, tampons, children's toys, wads of toilet paper, and balls of hair, grease, oil, table scraps, clothing, rags, sand, dirt, rocks, or newspapers. Tenants agree to pay for clearing the drains of any and all stoppages except those which the plumber who is called to clear the stoppage will attest in writing were caused by defective plumbing, tree roots, or covered by insurance.

TRASH - Tenants agree to dispose of their ordinary household trash by placing it into a receptacle for periodic collection. They agree to dispose of their extraordinary household trash, such as Christmas trees, damaged furniture, broken appliances, and the like, by compacting it so that it will fit inside their trash receptacle or by hauling it to the dump themselves or by paying someone else to haul it away.

DAMAGE - Tenants agree to pay for repairs of all damage that they or their guests have caused.

LOCKS - Tenants agree that they will not change the locks on any door or mailbox without first obtaining Owners' written permission. Having obtained permission, they agree to pay for changing the locks themselves and to provide the Owners with one duplicate key per lock.

LOCKOUTS - Should Tenants lock themselves out of their dwelling and be unable to gain access through their own resources, they may call upon a professional locksmith or the manager to let them in. In either case, they are responsible for payment of the charges and/or damages involved. Management charges a fee of fifteen dollars ($15) for providing this service between the hours of 8 a.m. and 6 p.m., Monday through Saturday, excepting holidays, and a fee of twenty-five dollars ($25) at other times. This fee is due and payable when the service is provided.

LANDSCAPING - Tenants agree to maintain the existing landscaping by watering, weeding, fertilizing, mowing, and shaping it as necessary. Additionally, Tenants agree to remove all snow from the driveway and sidewalks during the winter months.

_____

Tenant

_____

Owners/Managers

ALTERATIONS, DECORATIONS, AND REPAIRS - Except as provided by law, Tenants agree not to alter or decorate their dwelling without first obtaining Owners' written permission. Decorations include painting and wallpapering. Further, Tenants agree not to repair their dwelling or anything belonging to the Owners without first obtaining Owners' written permission unless such repairs cost less than one hundred dollars ($100), and Tenants agree to pay for them. Tenants shall hold Owners harmless for any contractors' liens or proceedings which Tenants cause. When approved by Owners, Tenants' plans for alterations and decorations shall bear a determination regarding ownership. If Tenants are able to convince Owners that Tenants can remove the alterations or decorations and restore that part of their dwelling to its original condition, then Owners may grant Tenants the right to remove them. Otherwise, any alterations or decorations made by Tenants become the property of Owners when Tenants vacate.

PAINTING - Owners reserve the right to determine when the dwelling will be painted unless there is any law to the contrary.

ACCESS - Owners recognize that Tenants have a right to privacy and wish to observe that right scrupulously. At certain times, however, Owners, their employees, or agents may have to gain access to the Tenants' dwelling for purposes of showing it to prospective Tenants, purchasers, lenders, or others or for repairs, inspection, or maintenance. When seeking access under ordinary circumstances, Owners will schedule entry between the hours of 8 a.m. and 8 p.m., Monday through Saturday, excepting holidays, and Owners will provide Tenants reasonable notice of twenty-four hours or less than twenty-four hours notice with Tenants' concurrence. In emergencies, there will be no notice.

PEACE AND QUIET - Tenants are entitled to the quiet enjoyment of their own dwelling, and their neighbors are entitled to the same.

Tenants agree that they will refrain from making loud noises and disturbances, that they will keep down the volume of their music and broadcast programs at all times so as not to disturb other people's peace and quiet, and that they will not install wind chimes.

TELEPHONE - If and when Tenants install a telephone in their dwelling, they will furnish Owners with the number within five calendar days. When divulging the number, Tenants shall advise Owners whether the number is listed or unlisted. If it is unlisted, Owners agree to take reasonable precautions to keep it from falling into the hands of third parties.

PROLONGED ABSENCES - Tenants agree that they will notify Owners whenever they plan to be absent from their dwelling for more than ten (10) days.

_____
Tenant

_____
Owners/Managers

94

LAWFUL USE - Tenants agree that they will not themselves engage in any illegal activities on the premises nor will they allow others to engage in any illegal activities on the premises insofar as they have the power to stop such activities.

INSURANCE - Owners have obtained insurance to cover fire damage to the building itself and liability insurance to cover certain personal injuries occurring as a result of property defects or owner negligence. Owners' insurance does not cover Tenants' possessions or Tenants' negligence. Tenants shall obtain a Renters' insurance policy to cover damage to or loss of their own possessions, as well as, losses resulting from their negligence. Tenants agree to name Owners as an additional insured party to the Renter's Insurance Policy. Tenants agree to show Owners evidence of such a policy within one (1) month from the date of this Agreement.

NSURANCE CONSIDERATIONS - Tenants agree that they will do nothing to the premises nor keep anything on the premises that will result in an increase in the Owners' insurance policy or an endangering of the premises. Neither will they allow anyone else to do so.

SMOKE DETECTORS - Tenants shall be responsible for ensuring that existing smoke detectors are in continual working order, including the replacement of batteries, as needed. If the smoke detectors become damaged or otherwise inoperable, Tenants shall immediately notify Owners in writing and be responsible for the replacement of smoke detectors under provisions of the repair clause herein.

RULES AND REGULATIONS - Owners' existing rules and regulations, if any, shall be signed by Tenants, attached to this Agreement, and incorporated into it. Owners may adopt other rules and regulations at a later time provided that they have a legitimate purpose, not modify Tenants' rights substantially, and not become effective without notice of at least two (2) weeks.

SERVICE OF PROCESS - Every Tenant who signs this Agreement agrees to be the agent of the other Tenants and occupants of this dwelling and are both authorized and required to accept, on behalf of the other Tenants and occupants, service of summons and other notices relative to the tenancy.

IDENTITY OF MANAGER - The person who is responsible for managing this dwelling and is authorized to accept legal service on Owners' behalf is N/A whose address is N/A.

CHANGES IN TERMS OF TENANCY - [This paragraph applies only when this Agreement is or has become a month-to-month agreement.] Owners shall advise Tenants of any changes in terms of tenancy with advance notice of at least thirty (30) days. Changes may include notices of termination, rent adjustments, or other reasonable changes in the terms of this Agreement.

_____
Tenant

_____
Owners/Managers

95

NOTICE OF INTENTION TO VACATE - [This paragraph applies only when this Agreement is or has become a month-to-month agreement.] When Tenants have decided to vacate the premises, they will give Owners written notice of their intentions at least thirty (30) days prior to their departure, and they will give an exact date when they expect to be moved out completely.

HOLDING OVER - If Tenants remain on the premises following the date of their termination of tenancy, they are "holding over" and become liable for "rental damages" equaling one-thirtieth (1/30th) of the amount of their then current monthly rent for every day they hold over.

POSSESSION - Owners shall endeavor to deliver possession to Tenants by the commencement date of this Agreement. Should Owners be unable to do so, they shall not be held liable for any damages Tenants suffer as a consequence, nor shall this Agreement be considered void unless Owners are unable to deliver possession within ten (10) days following the commencement date. Tenants' responsibility to pay rent shall begin when they receive possession.

ILLEGAL PROVISIONS NOT AFFECTING LEGAL PROVISION - Whatever item in this Agreement is found to be contrary to any local, provincial, or federal law shall be considered null and void, just as if it had never appeared in the Agreement, and it shall not affect the validity of any other item in the Agreement.**NON-WAIVER** - Should either Owners or Tenants waive their rights to enforce any breach of this Agreement, that waiver shall be considered temporary and not a continuing waiver of any later breach. Although Owners may know when accepting rent that Tenants are violating one or more of this Agreement's conditions, Owners in accepting the rent are in no way waiving their rights to enforce the breach. Neither Owners nor Tenants shall have waived their rights to enforce any breach unless they agree to a waiver in writing.

REFERENCES IN WORDING - Plural references made to the parties involved in this Agreement may also be singular, and singular references may be plural. These references also apply to Owners' and Tenants' heirs, executors, administrators, or successors, as the case may be.

ENTIRE AGREEMENT - As written, this Agreement constitutes the entire agreement between the Tenants and Owners. They have made no further promises of any kind to one another, nor have they reached any other understandings, either verbal or written.

ACKNOWLEDGMENT - Tenants hereby acknowledge that they have read this Agreement, understand it, agree to it, and have been given a copy.

_____
Tenant

_____
Owners/Managers

RENTAL APPLICATION - Tenants warrant and represent that the information and statements provided in the rental application signed by Tenants are true and that such application is incorporated herein by reference as though fully rewritten herein. If any information or statement contained in said application is found to be false, Owner shall have the right to terminate this lease by giving Tenants three (3) days' prior notice.

LIMITATION OF OWNER'S LIABILITY - In the event of any transfer of title to the leased premises, from and after such transfer, Owner shall be released from all obligations under this lease accruing after the date of transfer. The transferee of title shall thereafter be deemed to have assumed all obligations of the Owner hereunder accruing on and after the date of transfer of title.

_____ _____
Owners/Managers   DATE:

_____ _____ _____
Tenants   DATE:

_____ _____
LEASE AGREEMENT

Option to Purchase Agreement

Made in this _____ day of _____, 20_____.

BETWEEN: _____ (Hereinafter called the "**LANDLORD**")
And _____ (Hereinafter called the "**TENANTS**")

WHEREAS the Landlord is the owner of the property hereinafter described;

AND WHEREAS the Landlord is desirous to rent the property to the Tenants;

AND WHEREAS the Tenants wish to enter into an agreement whereby at specified times during the rental term, they have the option to purchase the property;

AND WHEREAS the parties have agreed to an option fee to ensure the Tenants have the opportunity to purchase the property after the first (1st) year of the term;

NOW THEREFORE FOR GOOD AND VALUABLE CONSIDERATION the receipt and sufficiency of which is hereby duly acknowledged and in consideration of the mutual covenants and agreements contained herein, the parties hereby covenant and agree as follows.

1. The Tenants shall have the right to purchase the property municipally identified as

    _____

    From **(insert date)** through **(insert date)**, for fixed price of $**(insert price)** provided that the tenants honor all other terms of their lease agreements with the Landlord. Tenants shall also have the right to purchase the dwelling from **(insert date)** through **(insert date)** for a fixed price of $**(insert price),** if notice in writing is given to the Landlord ninety (90) days prior to the completion of the term of the Lease Agreement attached in Schedule "A" and on the following terms and conditions.

    _____

    Tenant

    _____

    Landlord

98

2. The Tenants submit the sum of $_____(**Down Payment**) made payable to the Landlord on the execution of this option representing a non-refundable option consideration ("Non-refundable Option Consideration") to be used towards the down payment of the purchase price without interest upon exercise of this option. In the event that the Tenants do not exercise this option or in the event of breach by the Tenants of this option or the Lease Agreement the Non-refundable Option Consideration is forfeited to the Landlord. The Tenants acknowledge that the Non-refundable Option Consideration is an option fee and not a rental deposit.

3. For each month that rent is paid per the Lease Agreement, the Tenants will earn a monthly credit ("Monthly Credit") of $_____ (**Credit**) towards the down payment of the purchase price of the Property. This credit will accrue to a maximum credit of $_____ (**Credit**) to be used towards the down payment of the purchase price without interest upon exercise of this option. The Tenants acknowledge that rent must be paid on time to earn the monthly credit. In the event that the Tenants do not exercise this option or in the event of breach by the Tenants of this option or the Lease Agreement the Monthly Credit is to be forfeited to the Landlord. The Tenants acknowledge that the Monthly Credit is an option fee.

4. During the term of the Lease Agreement the Landlord shall pay and discharge all taxes, levies, fees and assessments and the Tenant shall perform any work orders issued as against the Property by any municipal, provincial and federal decision-making body.

5. If the Tenants abandon the Property for any reason whatsoever this option becomes null and void. If default occurs pursuant to the Lease Agreement or the Tenants fail to perform the provisions of the Lease Agreement the Landlord may declare this option null and void by thirty (30) days written notice to that effect personally served upon the Tenants or mailed in a registered letter addressed to the Property and upon the expiration of the time in the said notice the rights and interests hereby created and existing in favour of the Tenants shall forthwith cease and the Tenants shall forfeit the Non-refundable Option Consideration and the Monthly Credit.

6. An assignment of this option is invalid unless approved by the Landlord and no agreement or conditions or relations between the Tenants and an assignee or any other person acquiring a right or interest from or through the Tenants shall preclude the Landlord from the right to convey the Property to the Tenants on the surrender of this option.

7. The Tenants covenant that he or she shall not advertise or list or enter into an agreement of purchase and sale to sell the Property prior to the closing of the transaction between the Landlord and Tenants entered into pursuant to the exercise of this option or in any manner convey its interest in the Property without the Landlord's prior written approval in the Landlord's sole discretion.

_____
Tenant

_____
Landlord

99

8. The Tenants acknowledge that registration against title to the Property of any notice or other reference to this option or the Tenants' interest in the Property is likely to prejudice and inconvenience the Landlord and potentially impede financing involving the Property. The registration or recording of this option shall result in the revocation or termination of this option by the Landlord and all monies paid to Landlord by the Tenants including but not limited to the Non-refundable Option Consideration and the Monthly Credit shall be retained by the Landlord as liquidated damages. The Tenants hereby agree to remove the registration at his/or her sole expense.

9. The parties acknowledge that the Landlord's actual damages are difficult to determine and that the Landlord is entitled to injunctive relief.

10. The closing of an agreement of purchase and sale between the Landlord and the Tenants entered into pursuant to the exercise of this option must occur within thirty (30) days from the expiration of the Lease Agreement.

11. No waiver of any provision of this option shall be valid unless in writing and signed by the party against whom enforcement of the waiver is sought. The failure on the part of any party to exercise and delay in exercising any right under this option shall not operate as a waiver of such right nor shall any single or partial exercise of any such right preclude any other or further exercise of such right or the exercise of any other right. The waiver by any party of any provision of this agreement shall not operate or be construed as a waiver of any other provision.

12. Any notice required to be given to the Landlord shall be delivered personally or mailed by registered mail to the Landlord's last known address or delivered to the Landlord via facsimile.

13. Any notice required to be given to the Tenants shall be mailed by registered mail to the Property or delivered to the Tenants via facsimile.

14. This option constitutes the entire agreement between the parties and any and all previous agreements, negotiations, discussions and understandings whether written or oral express or implied between the parties or on their behalf relating to the option are merged herein and shall be of no further force or effect. There are no representations, warranties, conditions, or other agreements express or implied statutory or otherwise between the parties hereto in connection with this option except as specifically set out herein.

15. This agreement may be modified or amended only in writing and signed by the parties and duly witnessed or it shall be void and shall have no force and effect.

16. If any provision of this option is held to be illegal, unenforceable or invalid, such provision shall be severed and be ineffective to the extent of such illegality unenforceability or invalidity and shall not affect or impair the remaining provisions of this agreement which shall remain in full force and effect.

_____

Tenant
_____

Landlord

17. Each party hereto agrees from time to time, subsequent to the date hereof to execute and deliver or cause to be executed and delivered to the other such instruments or further assurances as may in the reasonable opinion of the other be necessary or desirable to give effect to the provisions of this option.
18. All covenants herein contained shall be construed to be joint as well as several, and that wherever the singular and the masculine are used throughout this option the same shall be construed as meaning the plural or the feminine where the context or the parties hereto so require and that these presents shall extend to and bind and benefit the heirs, executors, administrators and assigns of each of the parties hereto. Any ambiguity in this agreement is to be resolved or interpreted in favour of the Landlord.
19. This option shall be governed by and construed in accordance with the laws of the Province of Ontario. The parties agree that Ontario shall be the jurisdiction to entertain any action or other legal proceedings arising from this agreement.
20. The parties acknowledge having read and understood the terms and conditions hereof and having obtained or been afforded the opportunity to obtain independent legal advice with respect to this option prior to its execution.
21. The Landlord agrees to refund the Non-refundable Option Consideration and the Monthly Credit if through the acts or omissions of the Landlord the Property is conveyed via foreclosure or power of sale or any other method taken to satisfy the Landlord's obligations to creditors of the Property.

IN WITNESS WHEREOF this agreement has been executed by the parties hereto effective as of the date first set forth above.
SIGNED, SEALED AND DELIVERED

_____
Tenant

_____
Tenant

_____
Landlord

_____
Landlord

101

Step # 9 - Additional Funds and Signed Agreements

Before you sit down to meet with your future tenants make sure that you are familiar with each clause in the agreement. You do not need to have it memorized. What I usually do is go over each of the important clauses on each page with them and have them read over the rest on their own if they need to.

Call to confirm the time that you will be meeting and that they will have a certified cheque or money order made payable to you. At this meeting, you will want to receive a substantial amount of money, preferably their full down payment portion.

There are a few different ways of doing this however this is what I normally require at each of our meetings prior to them receiving the keys.

At each meeting there should be a fair exchange.

Meeting #1

Owner: Sign lease and option to purchase agreements (2 copies of each) and give them a copy for their records.

Future Homeowner: hand over full Option Fee (down payment).

103

When the meeting begins have them look over the agreement and explain all of the major clauses in the agreement. As I mentioned earlier, you do not need to go through it word for word but it is important that you highlight the major points.

Let them know that you prefer open communication, especially if they are going to be late with their rent payment. Remember, this is a business relationship, not friendship. If they are late with their payment, it is important that you start the eviction process once the rent is considered late.

It is important to do this as it sets the tone. They know exactly what is expected from them, how much the home costs is each year, how many credits they will earn, what happens if they are late with their rent cheque, etc.

At the conclusion of this meeting, make sure that you inform them to contact hydro, gas and water companies to transfer these utilities into their names.

Prior to your new tenants moving in, you will want to make sure that you visit your property at least one more time to remove your tables, chairs, furniture used for staging and any other items that may still be at the property.

Meeting #2

Owner: Hand over keys to the property.

Future Homeowner: Provides additional funds (usually first and last month's rent) and postdated cheques to the end of the calendar year (i.e. December).

For instance, your tenant moves into the property in August. You ask them for first and last month, plus postdated cheques to December. Why? This makes your year-end process much easier when it comes to collecting additional postdated cheques for the upcoming year. If you have multiple properties, it especially helps to streamline processes, banking and bookkeeping.

For all postdated cheques and down payment you have received, ensure you have taken copies.

Visit your bank where your new account is set up and ask them to deposit your postdated cheques on the first of the month. Expect the bank to charge minimal service fees.

> Another important step to remember at this meeting is making sure that all utilities have been transferred into their names (water, hydro, and gas).

Depending on the city where the property is located, the water bill may have to stay in your name (i.e. homeowner).

If this is the case, call the water company and have them add your tenant's name on the bill so that when it is mailed to your rental property they can open and pay the bill on your behalf.

If the water bill must remain in your name, make sure to call the water company from time to time to make sure the tenant is making timely payments.

Get to Know Them

Before I hand them the keys to their new home, I like to get to know them. I like to know what they like to do, what their favourite restaurants are and other personal details. There are a couple reasons why I do this:

1. It allows me to get to know them better.
2. It helps me to determine an appropriate gift to present to them when they move in.

I usually leave a $100 gift card to a restaurant they said they like, a mall they like shopping at or for a night out at the movies. This gesture helps strengthen the relationship by showing the future homeowner that you are thoughtful and considerate. In turn, the future homeowner is encouraged to do the same. It sets a great tone right at the beginning of the relationship.

Remember, they are paying down your mortgage each and every month. A $100 gift is not a lot of money in the grand scheme of things.

I usually leave this in the home on the kitchen counter in a nice Thank You note or by a basket of flowers.

Once you hand them the keys to the house, let them know that you will be in contact with them in a few weeks to see how things went with the move and to discuss working with them on any credit issues they may have with your mortgage broker.

Document Your Home's Condition

Prior to them moving in, it is a good idea to take as many pictures as you can of your property. I do this to have proof of what the property looked like prior to their moving in. For most of my homes, I do a video walkthrough which is a great way of properly documenting the condition of your home prior to occupancy as it provides evidence if you should ever need it.

You always want to make sure to properly protect yourself, especially when you are dealing with an expensive investment such as a home.

Tenant Selection is the Key

By working with clients who have been previous homeowners, who are putting down a substantial amount of money and are serious about getting into home ownership you are creating a win/win scenario, minimizing risk, as they value home ownership. They are not simply tenants.

Because of our stringent selection process, problematic tenant issues are virtually non-existent.

Recap

In each meeting there should be a fair and equal exchange. In the first meeting you are promising them the home if they fulfill the rest of the agreement once additional funds are received. The future homeowner is providing you with a portion of their full deposit.

In the second meeting they hand over the rest of the funds and you give them the keys to the property. It is important to always get a certified cheque or a money order.

Very important step: make sure the funds have cleared!

When meeting with the tenants I prefer meeting them at the home or at a coffee shop. **Do not** meet with them at your home.

I meet most of my tenants at the home they are about to move into. Since I'm buying beautiful homes in beautiful neighbour hoods it gives them a second viewing of the home and reconfirms that they've made the right choice.

If you follow the process, it is not difficult at all and it sets the tone of the relationship.

Should the tenants ever decide to leave, you have received a non-refundable deposit that will help offset any carrying costs you may incur.

Step #10 - After They Move In

Step 1. Send Them a Congratulations E-mail

Below is an e-mail I typically send out to my tenants, which you can use as a guideline.

Congratulations _____ and welcome to your new home! You are on your way to home ownership; you've made the Smart Choice!

Now that you'll be moving into your new home there are a few things that we want you to know about Rent to Own and the additional services we provide that allow us to stand above the crowd.

The MOST Important Step

Once you've moved into your home and settled in, please contact us to arrange a one-on-one consultation with our mortgage lending specialist who will assist you in restoring your credit to ensure you'll be able to purchase the home in the next few years.

Each and every month a portion of your rent payment (typically $200-$400, depending on the program) is credited towards your down payment. In other words, it's an automatic forced savings for you and your family.

Now, unlike regular rental properties you will be put in full control of the home for a specified period of time without actually owning it. You're free to paint, finish the basement, add a deck to the backyard, and more. The great thing about Rent to Own is you're spending very little to control a very expensive, and very profitable, piece of real estate. At the end of the agreed upon term, you'll also have a substantial down payment saved in order to purchase the home and transfer ownership into your name.

After your tenants have moved in, give them time to settle in and unpack before giving them a call. When you call them, let them know that it is time for them to contact your mortgage specialist to assist them in restoring their credit.

This is an important part of the program. If they have credit issues, you do not want to wait until the middle of the second year for them to try and get things in order. By then it will be too late. Credit restoration takes time and it allows them to know that you sincerely care about helping them into home ownership.

You will also want to visit your property from time to time to ensure that it is being maintained properly. I like to get out to each of my properties at least once every 2 or 3 months. It's a matter of personal preference, time management and priorities. Some people will tell you to visit more and others will tell you to visit less. Whatever you decide, it's important to visit your investment on a regular basis. After all, you have established an appreciation rate for the property, therefore it is imperative you ensure the tenants are maintaining and hopefully enhancing the property value as well.

Looking back on the first few Rent to Own homes I purchased, when I visited the properties I was pleasantly surprised. The homes were all in excellent condition, the lawns were being cut and some had already started to paint. I can't say the same for the first few properties I purchased that were straight rentals.

Winterizing Your Home

An important visit to make is during the autumn season. You will want to make sure that they are starting to winterize the home and all exterior hose bibs and valves have been turned off. Most of your tenants may know this, especially if they were previous homeowners. But new tenants to home ownership may not. Don't assume or leave anything to chance. Show them how to winterize the home, which will minimize risk and prevent any unexpected repairs or damages.

Tell them to make sure they are changing the air filter in their homes every 3 months. This will help keep the air clean, allowing for better air circulation and will cut down on the heat bill during the winter months

Mail

From time to time, you may have some mail that will go to your rental property. We usually inform our tenants to keep any mail that arrives and to let us know. We can then do a change of address with our local postal outlet.

Year-end

This is an important time of the year for you. This is when you get all your paper work in order, get ready for tax time and touch base with your tenants.

The first thing I like to work on is our tenant's annual statement. This statement is to show how many credits they have earned for the year, what months they received credits in and which ones they did not. To make things easier for you at year-end, have separate bank accounts for each investment property.

To determine this, I go through the bank accounts for each property. Here is a copy of the one that I use for my tenants.

Annual Statement – 201X
John & Jane Smith

Below is the total amount you have saved up to date to be credited towards your down payment for the property located at 123 Somewhere Lane –Any City, ON.

Total down payment received prior to move in date: $5,000.00

201X

January		Paid as agreed	$200.00
February		Paid as agreed	$200.00
March		Paid as agreed	$200.00
April		Paid as agreed	$200.00
May		Paid as agreed	$200.00
June	**Late**	Goodwill credit	$200.00
July		Paid as agreed	$200.00
August		Paid as agreed	$200.00
September		Paid as agreed	$200.00
October		Paid as agreed	$200.00
November	**Late**	***no credit earned	$0
December		Paid as agreed	$200.00
Total rent credits earned for the year			$2,200.00
Total down payment saved to date:			$7,200.00

Your monthly payments are currently $1,600.00 and will continue through to the month of December 201X.

Between the months of January 201X through to December 201Y the rent will be $1,600.00 as agreed.

The initial down payment in addition to the monthly saved credits will accrue and will be used towards the down payment of the purchase price of this home.

Our number one priority is to get you into home ownership.

The tenant acknowledges that the rent must be paid on time to earn the monthly credits. In the event that the Tenants do not exercise this option or in the event of breach by the tenants of this option or the Lease Agreement, the monthly credits will be forfeited to the Landlord.

_____
Tenant
_____
Landlord

Postdated Cheques

In November or early December, you will want to pick up the postdated cheques for the new year for another 12 months. By law the tenant does not have to give you postdated cheques however, it does help save time for both you and them. Most tenants agree to provide postdated cheques.

Gift Time

When dropping off the annual statement we also make sure to give our tenants a nice holiday gift as well. Some may feel that a gift is not necessary. We disagree.

This gesture is a token of appreciation and goes a long way in maintaining a strong and healthy relationship with your tenant.

A Few Tax Tips

This section is not intended to replace the advice of a tax specialist or an accountant. Providing extensive tax strategies is another book. However, here are a few pointers that have helped me to stay organized and get prepared for the annual tax filing project.

Create a paper file for each Rent to Own property where you can separate your documents (examples of headings: mortgage/tax/insurance, postdated cheques, agreements, utilities, home improvements, closing docs).

Keep receipts for any home improvements you have done to the property.

Make sure to open a separate account for each Rent to Own property. This is beneficial, especially at tax time to calculate rent, service charges and other related expenses.

On the following page is our POST TENANT CHECKLIST that we use after our tenants have moved in.

Post Tenant Checklist

After your tenant has moved into the property you will want to confirm the following:

☐ Has the tenant transferred all the utilities into their name? Confirm this with the utility company.

☐ Inform the tenant to notify you if any mail arrives.

☐ If the tenant has changed the locks on the front door/ garage, etc., ensure they have given you a copy of the keys.

☐ For all postdated cheques and down payment you have received, ensure you have taken copies.

☐ Create a file for your property where you can separate your documents (examples of headings: mortgage/tax/ insurance, postdated cheques, agreements, utilities, home improvements, closing docs).

☐ Keep receipts for any home improvements you have made to the property.

☐ If you have not opened a separate account for your property, do this ASAP. This is beneficial especially at tax time to calculate rent, service charges, etc.

☐ Visit your bank where your new account is set up and ask them to deposit your postdated cheques on the first of the month. (Additional bank service charges will apply.)

Congratulations You Did It
And some other important stuff

Joint Ventures

When you get involved in Real Estate investing, there will come a time when you run out of capital. Participating in joint ventures can be a great way to continue to grow your portfolio.

Like taxes, this topic alone could be a book in itself. It is important to exercise your due diligence before entering into a joint venture agreement with anyone.

So let me tell you about my own personal story, how I first started, and why I agree with carrying out joint venture agreements.

Several years ago, Darlene and I obtained our first rental property through a joint venture agreement. The property was a fully detached bungalow with a finished basement and a separate entrance. The lot size was 50' by 200' and we purchased it for under $200,000. It is almost impossible to find a home in the Durham Region of Ontario that is fully detached with an over sized lot for that price today, unless it is run down or not in a very desirable area.

You may recall that shortly after the recession of 2008 some interesting things were happening in the Real Estate market. For example, you could purchase a property with $0 down! That's right – no down payment. Sounds crazy, but it was true.

The only thing that was required out of pocket for this property was the closing costs and lawyer fees, which at the time totaled $2,943.86.

> Guess what, we didn't have the money to do it on our own.
> Embarrassing, but true.

A Joint Venture agreement allowed us to get started in Real Estate. If we knew then what we know now; we would have purchased 10 homes that year.

Whether you are looking to purchase your first investment property or already have 10 homes in your back pocket, there will come a time when you will eventually exhaust your capital. When you do, you will need to turn to a partner to help increase your wealth and cash flow. Joint venture agreements are a viable alternative.

Most joint venture agreements work like the one on the next page, however, they can come in a number of different varieties.

Investor A has the money but no time and wants to start investing into Real Estate. Investor B has no capital to invest but has the experience or is willing to manage the property.

The key is that there has to be a benefit to each joint venture partner for it to work. Investor A needs something from investor B and vice-versa and it's a 50/50 split right down the middle. Now there are obviously other ways joint venture agreements can be formed. You can do a 60/40 or 70/30 because someone is bringing more to the table, but 50/50 is the one that I tend to see transpire most often.

Each Joint Venture agreement can be different, so I always recommend that you have your lawyer look over the agreement to make sure it fits your needs and protects your interest and investment.

JOINT VENTURE AGREEMENT

THIS JOINT VENTURE AGREEMENT is made as of the xxxxxxxxxxxxxxxx 201X by and among xxxxxxxxxx, xxxxxxxxxx, xxxxxxxxxx and xxxxxxxxxx.

1. **AGREEMENT OF JOINT VENTURE**
   The Venturers hereby form a joint venture for the limited purpose and scope set forth in this Agreement. **xxxxxxxxxx, xxxxxxxxxx, xxxxxxxxxx** and **xxxxxxxxxx** are the sole Venturers of the Joint Venture.

2. **STATUTORY COMPLIANCE**
   The Venturers shall comply with the Federal laws of Canada as applicable and such Provincial legislations that may be applicable.

3. **PURPOSE** .
   The Joint Venturers have agreed to make contributions to a common fund for the purpose of acquiring and holding: **xxxxxxxxxxxxxxxxxxxxxx xxx-xxx** called the business interest.

4. **TERM OF THE JOINT VENTURE**
   The term of the Joint Venture shall commence on and as of the date of this Agreement and shall continue until the property is sold.

5. **PLACE OF BUSINESS**
   The principal place of business of the Joint Venture shall be **xxxxxxxxxxxxxxxxxxxxxx xxx-xxx** or such other place or places as the Venturers may from time to time select.

6. **VENTURERS**
   The Venturers and their respective addresses, initial investments in monetary terms for the purposes of calculating their accounts are set forth as below:

Name of Joint Venturer	Contribution
xxxxxxxxxxxxxxx	25%
xxxxxxxxxxxxxxx	25%
xxxxxxxxxxxxxxx	25%
xxxxxxxxxxxxxxx	25%

7. **REPRESENTATIONS AND WARRANTIES**

7.1 Each Venturer represents and warrants to the other Venturers that as of the date hereof:

a) It is in good standing and has all the requisite power and authority to enter into this Joint Venture Agreement;

b) That such Venturer has all requisite power and authority and approval required to enter into and execute and deliver this Agreement and to fully perform its obligations hereunder;

c) That each Venturer has taken all actions necessary to authorize it to enter into and perform its obligations under this Agreement and this Agreement is a legal, valid and binding obligation of the Venturer enforceable against such Venturer in accordance with its terms.

8. **NO CONSENT.** No authorization, approval or consent of any person is required in connection with such Venturer's execution and delivery of this Agreement and performance of its obligations thereunder. In the event such consent is required the Venturer undertakes to immediately proceed to obtain such consent.

9. **ALLOCATION OF NET PROFITS FOR TAX PURPOSES AND NET LOSSES FOR TAX PURPOSES**

The Venturers and each of them covenant and agree that their portion of the profit shall be treated in accordance with such laws of the Province in which they are located or incorporated as may apply and such Federal laws of Canada as may apply. The execution of this Agreement shall not be deemed to be either an acknowledgement or agreement that such bodies shall have any type of taxing authority.

10. **BOOKS, RECORDS, ACCOUNTING AND REPORTS**

The Joint Venture's books and records, together with all the documentation and papers pertaining to the Joint Venture Business shall be kept at the principal place of business of the Joint Venture. As well, a duplicate copy of the books will be available at the offices of the Joint Venture at **xxxxxxxxxxxxxxxxxxxxxxxxx xxx-xxx**. On or before the **xxxxxxxxxxxxxxxxxx** in each year, the Venture shall cause to be prepared by the Joint Venture's independent accountants and delivered to each Venturer as the expense of the Joint Venture, an annual report of the Joint Venture related to the preceding fiscal year containing an audited balance sheet, profit and loss and cash flow statements.

11. **BANK ACCOUNTS**

All funds belonging to the Joint Venture shall be deposited in the name of the Joint Venture in such bank account or accounts as shall be determined by the Venturers. All withdrawals there from shall be made upon cheques signed on behalf of the Joint Venturers.

12. **OTHER BUSINESS VENTURES**

The Joint Venturers and their affiliates may hereafter engage or possess any other business, investment or activities of any nature and description, independently or with others and neither the Joint Venture nor any of the Venturers shall have any rights in or to the said other business. None of the Venturers shall have any obligation to present any business opportunities to the Joint Venture even if such business opportunity is of a character consistent with the Joint Venture business.

The Joint Venture expressly waives the right to claim that any such business opportunity constitutes a Joint Venture opportunity.

13. **ADMISSION OR WITHDRAWAL OF VENTURERS**

Except as otherwise provided in this Agreement, a person may become a Venturer only with the approval of all Venturers.

14. LIMITED LIABILITY OF VENTURERS

Notwithstanding anything to the contrary stated herein, none of the Venturers nor any officer, director, shareholder, employees, agent, affiliate of permitted successor and assign of any of the Venturers shall be liable, responsible or accountable in damages or otherwise to the other Venturers or to the Joint Venture for any errors in judgement, for any act, including any act of active negligence, performed by such person or for any omission or failure to act, if the performance of such act or such omission or failure is done in good faith, is within the scope of the authority conferred upon such person by this Agreement or by law and does not constitute breach of fiduciary duty, breach of any representation, warranty or covenant contained in this Agreement, wilful misconduct, gross negligence or reckless disregard of duties.

15. DISSOLUTION AND LIQUIDATION OF THE JOINT VENTURE

15.1. *Events of Dissolution* .

The Joint Venture shall be dissolved upon the first to occur of the following events:

a) The expiration of the stated term of the Joint Venture

b) The written agreement of all of the Venturers;

c) The sale or other disposition of all or substantially all of the assets of the Joint Venture to one or more bona fide purchasers for value.

d) As otherwise provided by operation of law.

15.2 *Winding Up* .

Upon the dissolution of the Joint Venture, the Joint Venture shall be terminated. The receivables of the Joint Venture shall be collected and its assets shall be liquidated as promptly as is consistent with obtaining the fair market value thereof. Upon dissolution the Joint Venture shall engage in no further business thereafter other than that necessary to operate the Joint Venture Business on an interim basis, collect its receivables and liquidate its assets.

This Agreement shall continue to be binding upon the Venturers during such winding up period.

16. NOTICES

All notices, demands and communications of any kind which any Venturer may be required or may desire to serve upon the Joint Venture and/or any other Venturer under the terms of this Agreement shall be in writing and shall be served upon such other Venturers by courier or other means of personal service, by telecopy, or by leaving a copy of such notice, demand or communication addressed:

a) In the case of the Joint Venture, to the Joint Venture's principal place of business

b) In the case of each Venturer, to the address set forth in Section 5 hereof or by mailing a copy thereof by certified or registered mail, postage prepaid with a return receipt requested, addressed to such address.

Service of any such notice shall be deemed complete on the date of actual delivery. The Joint Venture and either Venturer may, by notice to the Joint Venturer and the other Venturers given in accordance with this Section, change the address to which all future notices to such person shall be made

17. GENERAL PROVISIONS

17.1 *Entire Agreement* .

This Agreement is the entire agreement between the Venturers with respect to the subject matter hereof and supersedes all prior agreements between them with respect thereto.

17.2 *Headings.*

The headings of the several sections of this Agreement are inserted solely for convenience of reference and in no way define, describe, limit, extend or aid in the construction of the scope, extent or intent of this Agreement or of any term or provision hereof.

17.3 *Severability.* In the event that any provision or any portion of any provision contained in this Agreement is unenforceable, the remaining provisions and, in the event that a portion of any provision is unenforceable, the remaining portion of such provision shall, nevertheless be carried into effect.

17.4 No Waiver .

The failure of any Venturer to enforce at any time or for any period of time the provisions of this Agreement shall not be construed as a waiver of such provision or of the right of such Venturer thereafter to enforce each and every such provision of this Agreement.

17.5 Further Assurances.

Each Venturer shall perform all such acts and execute and deliver all such instruments, documents and writings as may be reasonably required to give full effect to this Agreement.

17.6 Time .

Time is of the essence with respect to this Agreement.

IN WITNESS WHEREOF, this Joint Venture Agreement is made as of the day and year first above written.

Signature/Date_____

Signature/Date_____

Signature/Date_____

Signature/Date_____

Eviction Process

"Hope for the best, but be prepared for the worst."
~ Anonymous

In the event your tenant is unable to meet their monthly payment commitment, you will need to take immediate action. As mentioned a few times before in this guide, it is important to protect yourself and to know each process for every step of the way. Laws are always changing, so make sure to call or visit their website for any new updates.

The Eviction Process in Ontario

If a tenant is not paying their monthly rent, here is the process to evict in Ontario.

There should be no need to hire a lawyer as the Process in Ontario is very well laid out.

After filing the N4 (below) your tenant has 14 days to pay. After that, if they don't vacate the premises, you can apply for a hearing date at which point the tenant will be sent a notice to appear for the Justice of the Peace at the Tenant Board.

You will need a copy of your lease, records of payments (a small spreadsheet is fine) and any pictures of the property you have on file to show that it's in good condition.

Ontario Tenant Tribunal Eviction Process

http://www.ltb.gov.on.ca/

Step 1: Fill out and hand deliver the N4. This gives the tenant 14 days to pay.

Notice to End a Tenancy Early for Non-payment of Rent

Print & Read the instructions:

http://www.ltb.gov.on.ca/graphics/stel02_111622.pdf

Step 2: After 14 days complete and submit the L1 for a Tribunal Hearing Date. There is a $150 filing fee.

Application to evict a tenant for non-payment of rent and to collect rent the tenant owes

Print & Read the instructions:

http://www.ltb.gov.on.ca/graphics/stel02_111627.pdf

If the tenant does not leave the property after a judgment against them then the Tenant Board has Sheriff services that can go to the property to remove them (they drive large SUVs that say "Enforcement" on the side of them). We have never had to use this service but it does exist if necessary.

What Should I Pay Attention To?

Believe it or not, I don't have a crystal ball. What I do know is no matter how bad the economy gets, people will always need somewhere to live. The GTA (Greater Toronto Area) continues to lead the charge with one of the highest immigration levels in the world. As a result, this continues to drive huge demand for rental properties and vacancy rates in Ontario remain very low. Below are a few of the key elements I pay attention to when deciding on purchasing a property for myself and our investors.

Vacancy Rates

When deciding to invest in Real Estate, this is one of the first things to look at. You don't want to be an investor who can't get his property filled. So how do you protect yourself from this?

I buy beautiful homes in beautiful neighbourhoods. It's as simple as that.

Infrastructure

Pay attention to changes that are happening in your community of interest. Will they attract new families to the area? Are they expanding or extending the highways? Are they improving public transportation to make travelling more convenient? Is there new commercial construction, or any schools or hospitals being built in the near future?

Household Income

Another important factor to consider is the household income. If you decide to purchase a higher end rental property and need to rent it out at the higher end of the scale, will there be a demand for it? Our secret is to purchase a nice starter home under 10 years old. There is significant demand for these types of properties. There are always young families just starting out, so why not have a home ready and waiting for them to occupy?

There are always opportunities in any market. Stay focused on good communities that have employment diversity, a growing population and low vacancy rates. Once you've done your homework and applied our SHC Investor guidelines, it's time to acquire your first property!

History has proven that massive amounts of wealth have been created in times of uncertainty. You simply need the right investment. For me, that investment is Real Estate. One of the best things I stopped doing was listening to my co-workers on how to make money or why not to invest in Real Estate. I got educated, followed the golden rules above, started investing and never looked back.

Top 10 Things to Do For Rental Properties

I have acquired a lot of knowledge and experience over the years by following the footprints of other successful investors. The knowledge I have learned and apply each time to any new properties I've acquired, is not always clear to the new investor. One of the key success factors is to follow solid guidelines and establish good habits in order to minimize risk and maximize the return on your investment.

With that in mind, here is a list of the top 10 things to do when investing in Real Estate.

1. **Deposit All Your Rent Cheques**.
   One of the strategies I use to help free up our time is to have our tenants give us postdated cheques for the year and hand them into the banks. For a small fee they will automatically deposit these cheques into your account without you having to remember each and every month. Now, your tenants are not obligated to do this however, if they do, it's a huge time saver for everyone involved.
2. **Visit Your Property.**
   When investing in Rent to Own properties the maintenance is usually kept to a minimum since your tenants are responsible for minor repairs. Your tenants move in knowing they are going to own the home in a few years and are willing to maintain your home. With that being said, it's still important as an investor to visit your property from time to time since you still own the home.
3. **Set Expectations Up Front.**
   Set the ground rules up front and be very clear with your delivery. It is important that they know when rent needs to be paid and if it is not, you will officially notify them by proceeding

with the eviction process. It is important to follow this process to avoid things from spiraling out of control.

4. **Send Annual Statements.**

   At the end of the year for all of my Rent to Own properties I send annual statements of all the credits they earned for paying on time. If you have tenants that have had late payments and they see what they lost out on, it helps to re-enforce the importance of paying on time.

5. **Insurance.**

   There are many insurance plans for your property. Make sure that you get the right plan and enough insurance to cover your home by talking to your insurance agent. A well designed insurance package can protect you from losses caused from fire, storms, vandalism, and personal injury and discrimination lawsuits. Remember, it's all about minimizing risk.

6. **Give Them a Gift.**

   I'm big on this one! For each of my tenants, I give a gift valued between $50 to $100 at year end. This may sound like a lot but, how much of your mortgage did they pay down this year for you? After you take this into consideration, you'll see it's not much at all. If you are not big on gifts, then consider sending them an e-card or calling them on their birthday. It will go a long way in maintaining a solid relationship.

7. **Keep Your Receipts.**

   They all add up in the end…literally. Maximize your tax savings by getting into the habit of keeping all your receipts related to your Rent to Own properties. When you are investing in real estate, there are many expenses you can write off such as signage, telephone, photos for advertising, and much more.

8. **Have a Good Accountant.**

   If you are investing in Real Estate, make sure you have a good accountant. Don't attempt to do everything yourself. Let your accountant focus on accounting while you focus on investing.

9. **Keep an Eye on Your Accounts.**

   No matter how good your cash flow may be, keep an eye on your accounts. Make sure the appropriate bank fees are coming out, the taxes are accurate, your home insurance is correct and if tenant cheques bounce, you take immediate action.

10. **Take Action.**

    It is important to do your homework and have a good understanding of what you are getting yourself into. Once you have done that, just do it! You will make mistakes along the way, which is normal. It is a part of the learning process. I have made our share of mistakes, but I have learned, I have grown and I can now share my knowledge and experience with others.

Testimonials from Some of Our Clients

When you receive feedback from people you have helped to achieve their goals in life, it helps you realize that you are moving in the right direction.

"We are thrilled with the knowledge and service by Smart Home Choice Inc. They helped us with acquiring our first Rent to Own property. Not only that, they found us our Rent to Own homeowners who moved into the property in less than 3 weeks after our property closed! The entire process was very smooth and what we liked most about it was that they took care of everything while keeping us informed of the process. I would highly recommend Smart Home Choice Inc. for anyone wanting to venture into the Rent to Own area of Real Estate. Not only are you helping others in need, you are also building your wealth."

Terry and Marina, Ajax

I had been interested in investing in Real Estate for a long time but didn't have the knowledge or courage to take the first step. After attending one of the Smart Home Choice seminars I was hooked. The SHC team are knowledgeable, professional and available every step of the way. They helped make my first experience with Real Estate investing as smooth as possible. I have now purchased my 2nd investment property through SHC and already have a future homeowner ready to move in.

Thank you Smart Home Choice!!

Heather, Bowmanville

133

Smart Home Choice is the way to go for investments. This is our second home we've purchased and it's been nothing but great customer service and support. At first we were a bit hesitant with investing into real estate again as we've previously had a bad experience with renters. With the RENT to OWN model it's been a very positive experience. I encourage you to start investing today with the help of the team at Smart Home Choice.

Karen and Damien, Pickering

The End...Or Rather the Beginning

This is the last section of my Smart Guide to Real Estate Investing book, but it's the beginning of a new chapter in your life.

I leave you with the very first article I wrote when Darlene, Don and I first started Smart Home Choice.

"Turning 36 years old made me take a look around and talk to friends, family and co-workers and I realized that more and more people are second guessing where they are in life or in the direction they're heading. Now, I think that's absolutely normal. Where the problem lies is if you're at this point in your life, but you do nothing to change it.

Many people get comfortable in their jobs even though they absolutely hate them. Why? It pays the bills? It gives them a false sense of security? Basically, it gets them by for another 2 weeks... and then pay day again. What a rat race.

"You can't change your destination overnight, but you can change your direction". - Jim Rohn. That's such an important phrase. I suggest you write that down, and post in on your bathroom mirror so you can see it every day before you head off to work.

Don't get me wrong...if you enjoy your job, great. But if you don't, then take action. You can't do anything about the past, keep an eye on the future, but to make a difference you can only do it in the now. Right now! THINK NOW. DECIDE NOW. ACT NOW.

I know when I first got into Real Estate many people tried to talk me out of it. They would say, "My sister's aunt, uncle's, brother-in-law did it and lost his shirt." Can that happen to me? Sure it can. It's no different than going into your final exam, being unprepared and then finding out you failed.

I do my research before purchasing a property. Population growth, income levels, unemployment rates, transportation expansions and best cities to invest in, and ensure the property of choice has a positive cash flow. Once you have positive cash flow, you minimize exposure to market risk.

I recently attended a management course that I found extremely educational and the principles taught could be applied to everyday life. The one thing that really stood out was the ingenious way of creating SMART goals. This part of the 2 day course impressed me because it reminded me of our business. It stood out because it made sense. For everyone that knows me, I write all my goals down but what you may not know is I never really took the time to determine if it was a SMART goal.

So before I go on any further I should fill you in on what I mean by SMART:

- ***S*** *- Specific*
- ***M*** *- Measurable*
- ***A*** *- Attainable*
- ***R*** *- Realistic*
- ***T*** *- Time*

Interesting! So now when I write down my goals, I make sure they are SMART. For example:

"I will attain 3 more homes by March 31st 201X by holding monthly seminars to help other families reach their financial goals on their own or by joint venture agreements."

Let's break it down again:

Specific - *My goal is to get more homes.*
Measurable - *I want 3 more homes within a specific time frame.*
Attainable - *Capital*
Realistic - *1 home a month*
Time - *3 months*

If you're writing your goals down, way to go, you're half way there. But by making them SMART goals, you now have a blueprint to achieve them - a road map on how you'll reach what you desire."

"Obstacles are those frightful things you see when you take your eye off the goal."- Henry Ford

You now have the tools, knowledge and formula required to create financial freedom for you and your family. It is just a matter of whether or not you take action.

About SHC Investor

SHC Investor is the expert advice you need when it comes to Real Estate Investing. We will show you why Rent to Own is a much more profitable investment vehicle and how it differs from a long term rental. We pair investors (clients looking to use real estate for profit) and pair them with tenants (clients looking to get into home ownership). We do this by using Rent to Own as a vehicle for a win-win scenario for both parties. The difference with our company is we are with you from start to finish...from the purchase of your investment property to finding a suitable tenant.

Learn more about our services at www.shcinvestor.ca.

"We wish each and every one of you the best success in your adventures in Real Estate."

About Author Gary Hibbert

What do you do when your employment income plateaus, you are disenchanted with the proverbial 'cost of living' wage increase and your earnings are not aligned with your desired lifestyle?

You ask yourself the $15 Million dollar question:
Why are some people successful while others are trapped in the rat race?

The answer: Most successful people have one common thing in their investment portfolio -- Real Estate!

Following the last major recession Gary knew things had to change. He knew Real Estate was the answer, but he did not want to be a landlord (too many horror stories). Then he discovered the Rent to Own concept. At first he wasn't convinced. *Why would I want to sell my home after a few years?* But the more he investigated and studied the concept, the more he realized that to be successful in life you had to do this one thing... *the more people you help to achieve what they want, you can have anything you want!*

Rent to Own is a win-win scenario. In less than 3 years, Gary had secured and brokered almost **$15 Million** in residential real estate, and personally acquired over $3 Million in real estate investments – all using the Rent to Own program. He is inspired to teach others how to do the same, and to create wealth not only for themselves, but for enerations to come and hence the book Smart Guide to Real Estate was born!

If you are ready to step onto the path of financial freedom, contact Gary Hibbert at www.shcinvestor.ca

Recommended Reading and Other Resources

1. Tom Karadza, Nick Karadza and Rob Minton. Income for life for Canadians. Canada. 2008
2. Jim Rohn. Live an exceptional life. CD. Better Life Media. November 15th, 2004
3. Brian Tracey. Eat That Frog. CD. BBC Audio. 2002